HOPE DEALER

BY LUCY HALL
B.S., NCAC, CASAC

Published & Developed by Sunwise Media © 2019
Sunwise Media

ISBN 978-1-09830-315-0

A Foreword

Ri-Karlo Handy
CEO of Sunwise Media, Hope Dealer, publisher

My father is a veteran. For years he worked as a teacher and a juvenile probation officer. But his time in the military took a huge toll on him, his life, and his ability to be well-adjusted in this world. That deeply affected what kind of father he could be to my brother and I.

As many veterans have, he turned to alcohol (and more) to remedy his problems. At first, it was only the drinking at night. Each morning he would then drink what seemed like gallons of black coffee the next day, to appear straight and sober for his students and colleagues. Eventually, that routine broke down. That's when things got worse. Much worse.

When trying to find answers about how to help someone struggling with recovery, I never could find a definitive answer that really helped. On the internet, there were mostly links to rehab centers popping up with a bunch of generic information that was articulate and empty, as far as I was concerned. When trying to help my father, I just didn't know what to do. But thankfully, I knew Lucy Hall. I always saw her as an inspirational figure, but didn't know "how" inspirational, until I really needed her.

I met Lucy through my work in the entertainment industry. Entertainment was all I'd done since I was 14. I had collaborated with music artists on videos, created scripted and unscripted content TV shows, and even ran an original program for a network. That list can go on. But I had no idea that it was only a matter of time before my meeting Lucy, my needs and painful dramas around my father, and my career in media would intersect. All of these things were about to come together, in a very meaningful way, and directly determine my next project.

Lucy had become such an inspirational and informational resource to me, around helping my dad, I felt like she needed to be that same resource to a bigger slice of the world. She needed to be a resource for people who were just like me--people who were coming up with empty internet searches--just like I was when I needed desperate help to understand what was going on with my dad, and how to help.

At that point, I decided to develop a documentary film and book that would help all of those allies of addicts who did not have someone like Lucy in their life.

The documentary film, "**HOPE VILLAGE**," sheds light on the harrowing experiences of women who suffered from addiction, and their day-to-day journey to recover at Mary Hall Freedom House. It's an introduction for the general public, to understand addiction and the process of recovery. However, this companion book is a tool that holds specific answers to all the question we have when the disease of addiction shoves its way into our lives. The book was developed to answer questions like: A) How long does recovery take? B) What can I do as a family member? C) What can clinicians do to better serve the recovery community?

With this book, "***Hope Dealer - A Complete Guide: From Rehab to Recovery,***" we hoped to provide desperately needed answers that people couldn't find otherwise, plus educate people on the proper understanding of what recovery really is. We wanted to produce a guide for recovering addicts, loved ones, and people who work in the field of recovery every day. And we did. As you read, I hope Lucy's wisdom will deeply enlighten you, and inspire you to look at the issue of addiction, and recovery, through a completely new lens.

Thank each of you for joining us on this journey. Spread this helpful book near and far. I look forward to bringing you more guides and stories like Lucy's--with inspirational blueprints to eradicate the social ills of life, and make the world a better place.

* * *

Tommie M. Richardson M.D.
Georgia Behavioral Health Professional, Addiction Specialist

Greetings! My name is Tommie Mack Richardson, M.D. I am certified by the American Society of Addiction Medicine, the American Board of Addiction Medicine as well as a fellow of the American Society of Addiction Medicine. I have worked exclusively in the addiction medicine specialty for over 30 years and I am a member of the American Medical Association. In Hope Dealer, Lucy Hall has. written an extraordinarily honest, practical and compelling guide to educate the potential actual addicted individual, their significant others (including family) and the clinicians providing treatment to the addict and family unit. She illustrates how substance use disorders have their origins and the sometimes overlooked fact how they are intimately connected to the so-called process addictions, i.e., gambling, shopping, sex and food (either overeating or food restriction), "the eating disorders." In recent years, neuroscience has revealed that addiction in any domain is a neurophysiological disorder caused by chemicals in the circuitry of the numerous nuclei that make up the human brain. I have worked closely with Lucy as the medical director for Mary Hall Freedom House for over 23 years. As Lucy has demonstrated in Hope Dealer, addiction has many facets to its manifestation. Genetics or family history accounts for over 50% of the likelihood, then there are the adverse childhood events, i.e., sexual, physical, psychological, spiritual and emotional trauma, and then there is the environment, the overall sociocultural environment of the country, state, community, and family. The treatment program at Mary Hall Freedom House that Lucy has established is truly a nurturing environment that educates, nurtures and supports the patients as well as their families while they are recovering from the chronic, progressive, and fatal disease of addiction. Treating the addicted patient alone without involving allies is rarely successful. During treatment, the patients must learn to identify all of their triggers for using, and with help from clinicians, develop and internalize adaptive coping skills to combat every trigger. Functional MRI studies have demonstrated that it takes approximately 24 months for the chemical imbalance caused by addiction to normalize. It is vitally important to understand that there are cooccurring psychiatric disorders in many

patients who suffer from substance use disorders, and they have to be treated with expertise and medical providers that are specialists in medications and techniques to treat these cooccurring diagnoses. Mary Hall Freedom House has these specialists available through Lucy's affiliations with many generous and compassionate organizations in the metropolitan Atlanta community. Over my career in addiction medicine, it is clear to me that addiction is a very treatable disease and many patients recover and go on to live productive lives and help others achieve the same. As a society, we need to remove the stigma of addiction being a moral badness or weakness and follow successful models demonstrated by other societies. Make it financially feasible for addicts to get the needed help and medications that could save many lives and lift the burden from our criminal justice system. Lucy Hall has given us an intelligent roadmap to make this feasible. I believe that Hope Dealer will become a useful instrument to addicts, their families, treatment providers and our society. Lucy's pearls that she provides at the end of each chapter in Hope Dealer are invaluable.

* * *

Dr. Craig L. Oliver, Sr.
Pastor, Elizabeth Baptist Church
Atlanta, Georgia

Navigating the unpredictable terrain of addiction can be quite a daunting task for the addict, ally, and clinician alike. There are no cookie-cutter methodologies that can be engaged to fight back the maelstrom of addiction, but rather; one must align themselves with a recovery process that effectively works for them. Lucy Hall has masterfully rendered a resource tool by way of "***Hope Dealer - A Complete Guide: From Rehab to Recovery***" which can be used as a customized directional compass for traversing the often-obscured landscape of addiction.

As a pastor for over 24 years, I am well acquainted with the challenges that addicts and their families face as a result of their disease. I have seen addiction tear apart families and cause the implosion of seemingly otherwise indestructible relational infrastructures. Yet even in the worst of situations, when properly guided by an effective recovery program, I have seen the resilience of the human spirit enabling many to overcome insurmountable circumstances. In each of the cases of triumph, however, effective and strategic guidance was critical to their success.

Lucy Hall presents tactical guidance that speaks from every vantage point in the existential dynamic of recovering from addiction, which in essence provides true hope. Confidence that is rooted in anything other than intentional and calculated guidance is merely wishful thinking. Conviction and belief predicated on a proven strategic blueprint, however, is a plan for success. Lean into the principles presented in this highly resourceful book and allow it to guide you toward your success.

* * *

Debra Rasouliyan, Ed.S., LPC
Retired, Atlanta City Detention Center
Atlanta, Georgia

Having been invited on Lucy Hall's journey 22-years ago, as a colleague and community partner, I have felt an immeasurable honor to have shared many of her life's milestones, and witnessed her professional and spiritual growth, as well as her many accomplishments throughout the years. We share the same passion in serving the needs of sick and suffering addicts, both believing that, "women do recover," and that addiction is not only a physical disease but also a spiritual disease.

As a community partner with the Atlanta City Detention Center, Lucy welcomed the graduates of my in-custody substance-abuse treatment program to Mary Hall Freedom House, when other programs would not accept them, because they had children or were indigent. I knew that when my graduates were accepted into Lucy's program, they were cared for spiritually, physically, and emotionally--and that Lucy and her staff would love them until they learned to love themselves.

For anyone who is in active addiction, touched by addiction, curious about addiction, or has lost someone dear to them, as a result of this disease, or perhaps you can't understand why the addict "just can't stop using," HOPE DEALER will not only provide clarity and understanding to the disease, but will also guide you through the disease from the addict's viewpoint, the family/loved one's viewpoint, and the clinician's view point. It offers suggestions for intervention, but most of all, it offers HOPE for anyone touched by this disease.

The author's insight and knowledge of the disease of addiction is unparalleled, and implements a holistic and compassionate approach in her treatment interventions. Truly, a wonderful testimony and educational tool!!

How to Use This Book

IN THIS MODERN AGE, books are rarely read from beginning to end. They are read in parts. People see sections that directly speak to where they are right now, flip to that section and they indulge. That is not a complaint. That is good. We're busy. And there are certain insights and passages of guidance that we just need *now.*

Therefore, I've designed this book to be more of a *resource guide*--one you can come back to over and over to get what you need when you need it. I've tried my best to ensure that in whichever sections you dive-in, you will get a powerful takeaway for your journey.

This book is written for people in recovery, people in need of recovery, loved-ones, allies, and clinicians. It is also written for those who want to learn more about addiction to help turn the tide of this dreadful disease.

Whether you engage ***HOPE DEALER, A Complete Guide: From Rehab to Recovery*** cover to cover or in designated sections, I pray you eventually consume it in its entirety. There are beneficial gems of life wisdom all throughout its pages, no matter your station in life.

DEDICATION

To Mom:

You are my daily inspiration.
You are my daily call-to-action.
R.I.P. Mary Hall.

To Dad:

God rest his soul. He was a hard-working man. He took over and raised us like a champ when our mother died. He worked ceaselessly every day, Monday through Friday; he then drank most of the weekend. Sundays would come around and people would come buy liquor from his home reserves. These were my images of normalization growing up. But this man never failed us through thick and through thin. I am forever grateful and proud.

To Mary and Christian:

All my love. I pray that the mother I am today makes up for it all.

Chapter List

Chapter List

Introduction:

Hope Inc.

"My product is hope."
- Lucy Hall

INTRODUCTION:

Hope Inc.

I'VE FOUND THE WAY OUT. If you haven't heard of me, I'm sort of like the Harriet Tubman of addiction recovery. And my organization is truly the Underground Railroad for many. We rescue souls who want to crossover from a life of addiction-bondage to a life of recovery and freedom. By every definition, I am a walking miracle. And I'm surrounded by other walking miracles. Some of us were supposed to be dead. Some of us, our families outright disowned. Some of us were even legally forbidden to see our own children again. But today, we are productive and noble citizens in a society that largely wrote us off as irredeemable. None of us were supposed to be here--and yet--here we are. We're truly alive and we're thriving--all of us. We are back from the dead.

My name is Lucy Hall, and I'm a person in longterm recovery. I am a former addict who broke free from one of the most cunning foes known to man--the brilliant nemesis of illicit drug and alcohol addiction. When people ask me who I am today, I simply say, "A woman of God." That's not who I've always been. But on this day, and for the last 30 years, that is exactly who I am and all I care to be. You would be hard challenged to find another woman alive more grateful than myself. I've seen dark things that many have never seen. I've fallen to lows that many have never fallen to and never will.

However and regardless, with faith, I rise. I've been lifted, straightened, and stood up from the gutters of despair, desperation and hopelessness. Now I get to live every moment of my life lifting others--helping them stand their own lives up again, and sometimes I can barely believe it.

The life I get to live today seems completely surreal at times. When God saved me from the clutches of drugs and alcohol three decades ago, I heard Him clearly say, "Go back and get others." And so, I obeyed. From the moment I submitted to that commandment, I've been taken to glory to greater glory--then--to even greater glory. If you would have told me how my life would turn out on the day those police officers said to me, "You have the right to remain silent!" I would have never believed you. I am one who intimately knows GRACE to be a real and tangible thing. I'm a credible witness. Though I am not here to proselytize for any of the religions, I am here to edify the truth of the amazing possibilities available to every broken human being--especially those who believe there is no hope for them. There are doorways out of the dark grips of addiction by GRACE (and by knowledge).

This grace not only saved me (as the founder and director of the Mary Hall Freedom House Inc.), I watch this same grace (mixed with a little skill and technique) save countless lives and families every single day. So for those who want to understand me or my life today, I can put it in a little nutshell for you. "I save because I was saved." All day. Everyday. I pay it forward.

Our motto at Mary Hall Freedom House is this: *"We will love you until you learn to love yourself."* That's real. That's in everything we do. Love restores. Hope lifts. These are our two main tools. The freedom we promise at Mary Hall Freedom House is real. Hope is our product. Freedom is our promise. In nearly every city and state in our union, you've got people who are social workers, but we are "Hope Dealers." Hope *is* our social work.

Hope is the beginning of all things. We know that a person who has been suffering cannot truly reintegrate into society as a functional human being without hope. Just having the will to get up in the morning is an action predicated on hope. You must have a modicum of hope that *this day right up under your feet* could possibly be the day that will bring you something BETTER. It could be the one to grant you the prime opportunity to be

BETTER as a person or to HAVE BETTER for your life. And though hope is that first and crucial goal, the second one is faith. Hope is like the batter, and faith is like the cake. It takes the first one to bake the second one. Once you achieve hope, let me show you how to achieve faith. There is a science to this process.

See, I have an intimate knowledge of how the grips of substance abuse forms around a person. I did not learn it from a medical course or book. I learned from experience. I watched it form around me. And there's one thing that I know for sure; when people reach out to a particular substance to abuse, they do so from a place of hopelessness. People with hope don't abuse. People with restored hope don't abuse. People in secret despair abuse. Hope is everything. And you can't get a person to faith without any hope for anything. Therefore, as I'm loving you, I'm giving you hope that you too can stop using. I'm giving you hope that you can get out of the cycle of jail and recidivism. I'm giving you hope that you can get your children back and restore your family. I'm giving you hope that you can get a job, keep a job and excel at it. I'm giving you hope that what God has done for me, God can do for you too. I'm a living example--and hopefully a beacon of hope, for those who have lost their own.

Our counselors are trained to know the value of hope. Our counselors know that if you can get a person to this first plateau of *hope,* you can get a person to the faith they'll need to start moving the mountains of fear, mountains of anxiety, mountains of uncertainty, mountains of all those things that keeps a person paralyzed in substance abuse. This is why we are "Hope Dealers."

Though we are called the Mary Hall Freedom "House," I've always had this vision of a village. And it wasn't until this year that Mary Hall Freedom House was blessed to buy and have our own apartment buildings. Right down the street from our offices. We're in a lease/purchase arrangement with one building, and someone else donated a building to us. We have this program that is a whole continuum of care for recovering women and their families. It amazes me. Who would have thought? This is the ever budding fruit of my faith in God, who has guided me to this point.

My message to all who have come into our doors is simple. *If He did it for me, He will do it for you*. I was no more worthy of His grace than you. I had fallen to the lowest of the low. And now all the freedom I have, so can you. Trust me. Take my hand, and I'll get you there.

Let's begin.

Chapter 1

Who's an Addict?

"Addiction is about living in oblivion and constantly seeking the substances to maintain that oblivion."
- Lucy Hall

CHAPTER 1

Who's an Addict?

The life of a new addict should have the title: "Slipping into Darkness." That's what that life truly is. New addicts generally have no clue they are addicts. They're just slowly unraveling, oblivious to what is happening to them. That's because addiction is gradual, deceptive and cunning. You don't feel it devouring you. It's not like falling off of a cliff and then, *boom!* Addiction is like quicksand. It eats you centimeter by centimeter. It is falling into an abyss so slowly that you don't even notice until you're up to your eyeballs. Then it's too late. You're in. And now you're embarrassed that you're in. And then comes *denial.*

Illustration:

Oblivion is an important word in this conversation. So is *denial*. However, today I like to live with the facts of my life; I don't live in voluntary oblivion anymore. I stick to the sobering truth like my life depends upon it--because it does. When it comes to addiction... Denial kills. Sobering truth is what keeps me on point today. It helps me make better decisions. It helps me conduct myself and my life better. And here's one very sobering truth: *I have a disease called Addiction.* Just facts. No denying.

I recall the day that left me with absolutely zero doubt about that fact. One single event took me into a deep acknowledgement of my disease. I saw myself. I saw my disease. Clearly. It didn't happen in a professional setting. I wasn't attending a recovery class nor conducting one. I was attending a family cookout. It was the average cookout you see happening all across America in the summers--meaning there was food and alcohol everywhere. I was <u>used</u> to that, but I had no idea the cookout was going to turn into a recovery lesson I'd never forget.

One of my relatives sat down for a conversation with me. She had her plate of food, I had mine. We were looking forward to catching up. And during our little catch-up she casually grabbed one of those little miniature beers--*little nips,* is how I refer to them. She sat the *little nip* of beer right down next to her plate. I was a couple of years into my recovery so you'd think this wouldn't be a problem, right? But like I said, this disease is cunning and this disease is baffling. I remember how she innocently sat that little beer on the table and started chatting away, talking to me. It was so eye-opening because I was only partially listening. I couldn't concentrate on her because I started concentrating on the little beverage. It was just sitting there covered in beautiful condensation, shimmering and sweating under the sun. My relative was barely touching the little thing--talking and talking away--and all I could do was wonder how in the world could she just sit there for hours and that little beer nip still be on the table, barely consumed? It was amazing "to me." It seemed like a Houdini magic trick "to me." *How to NOT make a beer fully disappear.*

In my mind (meaning *my diseased neurology)* I kept thinking about how many of those little things I would have downed (just two years prior) in that same window of time. And she was just talking and talking and talking. She wasn't even thinking about that beer. But, *I was!* And THAT let me know I certainly had a disease. I had a problem. I wasn't normal. She was. I realized I had an extremely different thinking than *normal* people and therefore could never let my guard down around this disease. At that moment, if you could see the insides of my brain versus her brain at that moment, completely different parts of my brain physiology would be lit up like a Christmas tree. Hers wouldn't. Her brain would be relaxed and unfazed but not mine; I have an addict's brain physiology. I have to respect that, monitor that, manage that and treat that. It was a powerful moment for me. Though I was already years into my recovery on that day, that moment was a deeper level of admitting my addiction. Did you hear that? "Years into my recovery."

To my relative (the non-alcoholic) that *little nip* was just a beer. No big deal. To my diseased brain that thing looked like a damned glistening pot of gold--and for me, "Fool's gold." I wanted no parts of it. I want no parts of it. Like I said, I live in the sobering truth now. But if you can tell similar stories like this, and you haven't yet admitted your problem, you might as well come take my hand and let me help you get free. Acknowledge the signs. Acknowledge the truth. There is a lighted path out of the darkness of addiction.

Addict:

Just as there are stages to the advancement of cancer, there are stages to the advancing disease of addiction: *Beginning, Advanced* and *Full Blown Crisis.* Are you ready to admit to a developing problem? We can only manage what we have the courage to admit to. If you're even remotely wondering if you're an addict, here are a few questions you should ask yourself.

HONESTY & ADDICTION: THE SELF QUESTIONS CHECKLIST

1. What has honestly brought me to the pages of this book?

2. How often do I consume addictive substances?

3. What have been some of the consequences of my getting high?

4. What things have I've compromised due to my craving to get high?

5. Have my priorities around work, family and personal well-being shifted?

6. Do I now organize my life around when I can use, where I can use and how often?

7. When friends invite me out for a drink, do I make sure to have a few extra before I go--to be ahead of the group?

8. Am I using my craved substance (or activity) to medicate my true emotional state, or avoid the feelings and realities of my life?

9. Do I even have the sobriety of honesty to be truthful in my answers to these questions?

ON THE ROAD TO ADDICTION, the following are key definitions we should know:

Misuse – When you use a substance (or activity) in a way that is other than the recommended use, or outside of what the substance (or activity) was originally designed. For example: If we take a substance designed for another purpose and we're using it to relax, we're misusing it.

Abuse – When the substance (or activity) is being habitually misused.

Addiction – When the use of a substance grows beyond a habitual decision, becoming a compulsive activity beyond

> choice, a biological (or biochemical) need. For example: college kids enlisting a perp to buy alcohol for them so they can party and get drunk; that's misuse. If the kids start doing it every week, it becomes abuse. Later, if they can't stop doing it, every weekend or weeknight, it has become addiction.

Do you see yourself reflected in any of these descriptions? How did you feel answering those questions and reading those definitions? Were you slightly uncomfortable? Did you have a self-righteous reaction, mumbling to self, *"None of this is me!"* failing to see the relevance? Were you like a kid twitching in his chair after his or her mother asked if he'd broken the lamp in the living-room?

Regardless, if you're still stuck in the mud of denial, let me shout this fact: *You're not alone.* You can relax any shame, embarrassment or defensiveness. You're living amidst millions who refuse to perceive or acknowledge their addiction. Some even refuse to consider the possibility. There's a whole community of functional addicts at this phase--the denial phase--a global community. I used to be a part of that community until I woke up, healed up and cleaned up. All of us start from this phase. All have to find the courage to do that first hard pivot, that first step, that first "about-face." *Admitting.*

I am in no way, form or fashion here to condemn you. That would be like condemning myself. I'm here to help. I used to live right where you are. Sometimes it just takes a community--a group of people standing on the outside--to tell you what they are seeing gradually happen to you. They see what's going on with you better than you do. Your mind and vision are completely IMPAIRED by the substance or activity you're choosing to impair it with. Remember? You didn't want to deal with reality. You wanted to escape it. That's what the substance use is for. So you're no longer seeing reality as it is. And you succeeded. And now you have fallen into a different reality called the disease of addiction. And it might be more of a demon than the first thing you were running from. Your community sees what's happening to you. People notice. If you find yourself reading this because someone photocopied it, screenshot it, or left it for you to find, there's a reason. They're not crazy. They see something. They see that something has changed in you. They see something you could no longer keep hidden. *They see.* Do you?

Ally:

Let's talk about this. I need to say a few things here to help you understand your loved one, family member, co-worker or friend. I'm here to request your deepest compassion for them. Plus, I'm here to give you key information to help you do just that. Here is one big piece. The sobering facts? ***You might not be as different from them as you think.*** Shocking? Well, wait until you here the big facts coming in the next paragraph.

Facts: Everyone self-medicates. Everyone feels emotions. Everyone feels overwhelmed by them from time to time. Everyone employs coping mechanisms to deal with their negative emotions and the life situations that provoke them. None of us are exceptions to this rule. Some of us reach for chocolate, some reach for sex, some reach for that credit card to go shopping, some reach for plate after plate after plate of food, and some just reach for the remote control to binge-watch television for hours on end--but all have coping-mechanisms in life.

Remember that word "oblivion?" Like I said, you and I are not going to live in that word again. And the first part of that commitment is to no longer kid yourself. So, my questions are these:

A SECOND LOOK AT YOUR COPING-MECHANISMS

1. Is your coping-mechanism a healthy one or a destructive one?

2. If destructive, are you now addicted to that coping-mechanism?

3. Are you now compulsive and obsessive about that coping-mechanism?

4. Do you just "have to have it?" Be honest.

5. Do you find yourself unwilling to give up that coping-mechanism and the temporary good feeling (or the escape from bad feelings) it gives you?

6. Since you say you can quit it at anytime, why do you not?

My friend! I hate to break it to you, but, addiction is addiction--whether we're that one using hard psychoactive drugs to self-medicate or that one using hours of nightly television binging to self-medicate. Those are just facts. And isn't there reason to be concerned about ANY dependency or addiction? What are we really doing to ourselves, our lives and why?

Your loved one simply has a coping-mechanism too--a habit. It may be particularly destructive. It may be one that is illegal. But they have a compulsive habit that is getting the best of them just like you may have one that has too much control over you and your life. But we all have habits. And sometimes our habits own us.

When dealing with the person you love--whom you suspect is an addict--come from that foundation of knowledge and shared experience. We are all human and we all self-medicate in our way--good or bad. **Our goal with the addict who is destroying themselves, their health and their life, is to help them find coping-mechanisms that are healthy instead of unhealthy.** This perspective helps us to talk to our loved ones from a non-judgmental place--in a way they can feel we have no judgement in us about it. They need to feel safe to come clean, admit and get help.

Clinician:

There is a reason we always hear about stars dying of overdose. *Admitting to one's addiction* isn't easy for anyone, but for those who live under the social limelight, or have very public positions in life, it's a whole other level. For our VIP persons, stepping out of oblivion and facing the hard cold truths can prove extremely difficult. As professionals, we sometimes have to put in the extra compassion and the extra work to get them out of the quicksand of denial and firmly into the mindset of the first step:

---

1. We admitted we were powerless over alcohol (or drugs)--that our lives had become unmanageable.

– The First Step of The 12-Steps of Alcoholics Anonymous

I've found through leading our programs for years, some of the ones who still haven't quite come to grips with the fact that they are addicts, usually hail from the "fancier" parts of society. When they find themselves in a group dynamic, with other addicts from the "non-fancy" parts of street life, it's quite the rude awakening for them.

When this individual looks around the room and sees all the faces they might normally look down upon--(when riding past the rougher neighborhoods of America in their expensive foreign sedans)--it's harsh on their psyches. But everyone in our program gets in touch with the truth, gets re-examined--and if they're lucky, gets re-made. As professionals, we have the same policy for whomever is in that room; we aim for everyone's troubled soul to get served like a VIP. It does not matter who you are. We get real so that we can heal. And society's VIPs have a rough ride until they drop the need to be *important and superior,* and simply embrace the need to be "free" of this deadly disease.

Addiction is quite the leveling field for all. The real story of addiction obliterates stereotypes. Being rich, powerful or privileged can no more solve the disease of addiction than it can solve the disease of cancer. At Mary Hall Freedom House, addiction knows no VIP. Everyone in that recovery room is a V.A.P.--meaning a *Very Addicted Person.* Class, wealth or popularity is a non-factor. The affliction is the same and the solution is the same.

Not only must we and society rid our minds of dangerous stereotypes, but addicted persons must as well. Too many think of a stereotype in their minds when the subject of addiction comes up and conclude, "I'm not that." They mean that they are not the picture of the person they see in their mind; this makes them wrongly conclude that they don't have a serious addiction problem, and keeps them from admitting their addiction as deeply as they need to, to finally get free. As clinicians, we have to be more vocal and work against addiction stereotypes in our society. Let's tell the truth about the broad diversity coming through our doors.

Doing this work for decades has taught me that you cannot detect an addict via stereotype. Many people (just by appearance) you would never think their story is what it is. This includes a lot of VIP persons with supposedly fantastic lives. Whatever stereotypes we have for addicts we might as well let that go. At Mary Hall Freedom House we get women of every race, ethnicity, religion, socio-economic background and social status. We even get them from every continent--and get this--not all of the women appear broken-down or dilapidated. Plenty of the women are breakneck gorgeous. But when they come through our doors, they come to finally admit that they are completely shattered inside beneath that designer clothing. Again, addiction is quite the leveling field for all.

Recovery:

Do any of the previous sections describe you and your life in any obvious or subtle way? Are you afraid to search and deeply review your life for any similarities? Do you truly have the ability to be "honest" in your assessment? Would the people who really know you best agree with your answers?

Truthful answers or even the need to keep lying to yourself will tell you a lot about what's really going on in you.

Recovery begins the moment you've courageously admitted there's a need for recovery. Just that one admission is the first step in the other direction. If you're one who has finally and courageously confessed you're an addict, alcoholic, or in need of the process of recovery, applaud yourself. It's your first solid *blow* against this clever disease. Keep going. Join a recovery process now. This is doable.

RECOVERY PEARL:

"Admit and be free. Deny and stay trapped."

Chapter 2

Why Do People Abuse?

"It's never about the addiction.
It's about the wound triggering the addiction."
- Lucy Hall

CHAPTER 2

Why Do People Abuse?

When you see an addict struggling with addiction (and all that comes along with it), you're not looking at someone struggling with a character issue, you're looking at someone struggling with a neurological disease. You're likely looking at someone suffering from an unhealed trauma. From any reasonable point of view (after any intelligent analysis), it's clear that addiction is not about *character or will*.

A Harvard published study says The American Society of Addiction Medicine describes addiction as "a primary, chronic disease of brain reward, motivation, memory, and related circuitry." Shopping, sex, food, drink, and drug alike can trigger brain mechanics and biochemistry, which feed obsessive-compulsive behavior for someone with addictive brain physiology, including those who have inherited it. Think about it. No one *knowingly* chooses to be an addict. Who would *choose* to be an addict with all that comes with a life of addiction? It is an absolutely MISERABLE existence. Addiction is never about a "moral choice" or character. Addiction is about a person drowning in the effects of a neurological disease that has overcome them from within.

Illustration:

Some of the most fascinating research I've ever found on why we use psychoactive drugs, emerged from a famous 1980s experiment called "Rat Park." The pivotal study suggests humans, like rats, abuse drugs because of environmental and emotional conditions--as opposed to the chemical power of drugs themselves.

It all started when 1960s psychologists expanded their routine experiments on lab rats into a brand new sector--drug addiction. Rodents routinely kept in large metal containers with solitary housing units per animal--like prison cells in a cell block--were subjected to a gruesome but telling experiment. Reportedly these rats were hoisted and tied to the ceilings of their tiny units, then connected to tubing with catheters stuck beneath their skin. The tubes delivered psychoactive drugs on demand whenever test subjects pressed a lever. Reportedly these deeply addicted rats succumbed to compulsion, consuming copious amounts of cocaine, amphetamine, heroin and other to their detriment or death. Reports say it was these findings that were used to fuel a raging war-on-drugs--a war to purge these addictive substances from our societies and pulverize the black market supplying it. And this was all enacted or executed by aggressive, punitive, and sometimes deadly means. At that time, society feared their children or spouses becoming addicted drones like these rats reportedly became. From this one study, the War on Drugs went to a whole new level.

However, decades later, new researchers began doubting the conclusions these 1960s researchers reached. There was doubt the lab rats' addictions were purely due to the addictive chemicals they were ingesting. They began suspecting there was a whole lot more to the story. New scientists decided to conduct another *rat vs. addiction* experiment at Simon Fraser University. They seemingly wanted to test an arising hypothesis against the findings of the earlier study. After learning more about this highly social, industrious, and exceedingly intelligent rodent species, it became easy to imagine how a traumatizing environment could have possibly created a traumatized test subject. Placing any sentient being under nerve-racking circumstances could cause them to seek available chemical escapes from their misery.

Perhaps the solitary confinement--and arguably, tortuous treatment--compelled the drug abuse more than the chemical hooks within it.

In this new experiment, entitled "Rat Park," drugs were made readily available to a community of lab rats. The key word there is "community." These rats were not kept in enclosed solitary confinements. They were not locked in cold, tiny compartments, unable to roam. They were not tied to ceilings with catheters protruding from their bodies. These rats were allowed to mingle in common areas full of rat toys and enticing terrains for them to climb, hop and happily scurry all over the place. The rats were also given tons of access to the opposite sex, allowed to mate and endlessly procreate. And finally, these rats were given access to copious amounts of mind-numbing drugs.

Simultaneously, Rat Park researchers (reportedly including Barry Beyerstein, Bruce Alexander, Patricia Hadaway and Robert Coambs) took another group of rats and recreated conditions of the 1960s "Skinner Box" experiment. Reportedly the rat group kept in the 1960s style solitary confinement were given access to the same buffet of drugs. However (surprisingly or not), the unconventional results were compelling, if not astonishing. Reporting says that after repeating the experiment numerous times, rats kept in the highly socialized, playful, rewarding, seemingly happier "Rat Park" barely used the drugs available to them--while rats kept in solitary consumed psychoactive drugs in huge amounts. It's not hard to imagine why. But according to reports, that research was said to be dismissed, or, perhaps discredited by the establishment. Therefore its logic was not broadly implemented in the "War on Drugs."

Today, many more are looking at the same 1960s Skinner Box experiment and concluding it was the isolationist environment that catalyzed the rodents into addictive behavior. The highly publicized "Rat Park" experiment has launched a whole new arena of thought about addiction and "connection." Some researchers and scientists are coming to completely new conclusions about what addiction is at the core. Some are concluding the opposite of addiction is not truly sobriety but "human connection." That's big. These researchers are suggesting that healthy "emotional bonding" is the lynchpin to healing the root cause of addiction. Maybe that's why the addict to addict "sponsors" of the Alcoholics Anonymous program have worked so well over the years.

Further, they also suggest "unhealthy human bonding" can take place with almost any object, or substance (as a substitute), when there are no people with whom a human can deeply relate or create a healthy bonding. These bold new findings are truly compelling--(to say the least)--and they seem to overlay perfectly with what I've witnessed throughout my decades in this work.

Addict:

Recovery is the only road back to yourself and a life worth living. If I can recover from all of this to become who I am today, you can too. There is nothing wrong with YOU, but there is something very wrong with this disease. Recovery shows you how to separate yourself from it. Choose recovery. I'm 30 years into my life of recovery. I've been there, done that. I know the slippery slopes. I know the powerlessness. I know the pain and hopelessness. But more importantly now, I know the way out. I want to take the hand of every addicted person in the world, and show them that there's a way out of this thing.

When entrapped by this disease, it is really important to accept and understand that it is a brain disease, not a character issue. **It's an entrapment within a neurological compulsion until skillfully interrupted.** In this entrapment, we're gradually going from freedom of "choice" to "less choice" to "choicelessness." Ultimately comes the complete loss of freedom and freedom of will. So the main thing to recover is what normal humans take for granted: "the will to choose."

This entire recovery process is about the administration of choices--avoiding the choices that trigger addiction, plus retrieving your power of choice in a life of recovery. An addicted life starts from one unfortunate choice, evolves to worse choices, then later, leaves one with zero choices. And during this succession of choices, the brain's neurology is gradually changed--rewiring itself to reflect the new and unhealthy choice.

When repeated by habit, the new choices become a new hardwiring, a new "law" in the brain of that individual, etched into their physiology. By sheer biological momentum, the diseased brain (addiction hardwiring) gains influence over the will of the human, releasing stronger and stronger cravings for the repetition of the addicted choices--even to the detriment of the individual's health, quality of life, and overall wellbeing. That new hardwiring (a/k/a "addiction disease") cunningly topples the power of the human, leaving them in the grips of this neurological entity until they rediscover, recover, and re-administrate their power again--or die.

When we get drunk or get "high" on a substance or activity, there is a flood of dopamine and serotonin that overruns the thinking part of the brain. You've heard the phrase "stuck on stupid." Well, on these hard substances, there is the actual interruption of the brain's intelligence center. I can testify that it all becomes a perilous battle inside. But remember, it "is" a winnable battle, especially if you give it all over to the God of your understanding. You must seek something more powerful than self to help you get in front of this again.

Step 2 of The 12-Steps of Alcoholics Anonymous says, "Came to believe that a Power greater than ourselves could restore us to sanity." Recovery is part medical work, part spiritual work and part emotional-psychological work. But it works. And your life can work again.

Ally:

At the Mary Hall Freedom House, we teach a course called *The Neurobiology of Addiction.* We also teach a course called *The Neurobiology of Trauma.* We translate this information into laymen's terms that everyday people can understand. We even teach a course called *The Neurobiology of Brain Chemicals and The Love Connection.* That's because some of our traumas stem from super-toxic relationships and the bonding chemicals that keep us in them.

A deep knowledge of these things helps our recovering addicts rise above any inner self-condemnation that may be further contributing to the toxic emotional states which led them to abuse. This is a very powerful and important part of our recovery program and their recovery process. That's why we go in-depth. We detail what happens to the diseased brain as they go from misuse, to abuse, to out-of-control active addiction.

These things are also important for the ALLY of a recovering person to know. Knowledge of the neurobiology of addiction allows you to truly see the disease happening in your loved one instead of attributing what's happening to the character of your loved one. Society has trained us all to do that, including the person struggling. When you can separate the disease from the person, in your mind, you are in a much better position to help them. You are in a much better position to have the compassion needed to get through this. You are in a much better emotional position to endure the journey ahead of you.

Clinician:

At Mary Hall Freedom House, I've given one of our chief recovery philosophies an often repeated title: I call it "Inside-Out." It's based on the understanding that when dealing with a person in addiction recovery, you first have to remedy their inside issues to remedy their outside habits. Addiction has such a dramatic external manifestation, people often focus on the outer manifestations only--neglecting to treat the root from which the disease springs. That's a mistake. A huge one.

To discover best methods and practices as a clinician--as well as to constantly evolve them--I repeatedly put myself in the place of an addict in our recovery program. I'm always thinking of what would have helped me the most when I was going through the storm. I use this approach a lot with my clinicians. I say, "Imagine if I were in your care. If you are truly going to help me, you've got to know what is going on with me from the inside-out. Everything you see manifesting in my outside life is directly caused by how I see myself and my life, on the inside."

I drill this into my practitioners because it's just true, true, true.

Clinicians: If I'm the addicted person in your care, DO NOT REST until you know where I've been, what has happened to me, where I've been hurt, and therefore, where to help me heal. Find the pain that I am trying to medicate with this drug or drink or activity. Pull me out of the hole I'm hiding in and seal that hole up. This is what the work looks like.

To Recovery:

Conventional understanding of addiction is being challenged on all sides today. And perhaps it should be. I welcome it. Because what our societies have been doing around the issue of addiction has not been working. That much is crystal clear. New narratives, new findings and new approaches are starting to be noticed. (Just wait until you hear about the Portugal Experiment and their findings. *Mind-blowing.)* The world's viewpoint on addiction is burdened with too many stereotypes and misunderstandings. One of my CHIEF PERSONAL GOALS is to evangelize a new public understanding of this cunning and deadly disease. A new comprehension can foster new social attitudes toward addicts, plus revolutionize how we approach and innovate new solutions. The issue of addiction needs to be 100% medicalized and humanized instead of criminalized.

RECOVERY PEARL:

"It's never about the drug. It's about the pain
we're trying to kill WITH the drug."

Chapter 3

Gateway Drugs: Myth or Reality?

"Hell has a doorway."
— Lucy Hall

CHAPTER 3

Gateway Drugs: Myth or Reality?

Many romance the notion that recreational drug use is harmless. However, if addiction runs in your family--if the inherited addiction neurology is lying dormant within you--that romance can end in indescribable heartache. The casual or social use of drugs and alcohol is a totally different ballgame--for *YOU.* It's a severe gamble. One hit can totally change your life. The addict is ALWAYS the person who started off thinking they were in control but gradually and imperceptibly lost control. From innocent beginnings they slowly become powerless in the grips of alcohol or some type of drug. And it's sad because many times that user starts off saying, "I'm just doing this socially." *Isn't this what we say to ourselves?*

Illustration:

Hell had a doorway for me. It even had a name. She was my beloved cousin. A favorite. Still is. Her dad and my dad were brothers. She was the one niece who was closest to my father and her father was the closest uncle to all of us. She was always coming over. Excluding my two brothers who passed away from overdose, it was Marsha, Yvonne, Eloise, Dennis, then me. And in the mix, there was always my cousin. She had a tight relationship with almost everyone in my clan of siblings. She was around my sister Yvonne's age. We considered her one of us. She would come over on weekends all of the time and she was very easy to look up to. She was that kind of person you couldn't help but want to be around; she was so cool--cool with everyone and such a loving person. She was and is the "life of the party" type.

I remember one time my Dad and Stepmom went away to a family reunion or something. My cousin would stay with us whenever they would travel. Loving her as much as they did, they always tapped her to care for us young ones in their absence. She was trusted, vetted and part of our inner circle. On that long weekend, I remember her sitting outside on the bench where we often sat and hung out. I can still see it in my mind. I was the young kid. She was the older "cool" cousin. I was just watching her. She was a fascinating personality and I was just soaking it all in. I wanted to grow up and be as cool as she was. *Who wouldn't?* Everything she did was interesting, and that day she was sitting there doing something very interesting as usual. She was lighting up a joint.

Once she started smoking it, her face became even more fascinating behind all the swirls of pretty smoke. I curiously asked her what that was. I wanted to know what she was doing--what she was smoking. I knew that was no cigarette. She said, "I'm smoking a joint. Why? You wanna try it?" And of course... I piped up and said, "Sure!"

Boom. That was it. The hole in my heart had found a patch.

That one moment became a doorway into a whole life that was on its way to me like a speeding train--a life of hell, crime, drama, pain--a life that would nearly take my life and threaten to leave my daughter motherless. But how could I have known that then? To me, I was just hanging out with a favorite cousin. She handed it to me. I took a hit. And at this point in my childhood, I had already been sneaking a cigarette or two, or three, so I knew how to use it. I knew how to inhale. I drew that smoke into my lungs and it was over. I was a goner, as they say. I found a way to feel good when I wasn't feeling good. I was going to be chasing that damned feeling for a long, long, long time. It was my gateway. I was 13. Things were about to get a lot worse, and so were my drugs of choice.

Addict:

When you don't yet know any better, you take that hit or order that drink, because you want to fit into a social situation. Someone passes a joint and you're just sitting there, and it would seem awkward if you didn't hit it. And when you do, you think it's harmless. But unbeknownst to you, you've begun a subtle "chemical and psychological" chain reaction that can revisit you days, weeks, years later. This is not just a P.S.A., this is my life (and so many others). This is a confession.

After the event in the previous section, I was going to have to keep smoking more, and finding more intense substances to chase the highs I was becoming addicted to--to blunt the pains of the life--the one's that were already there plus the new ones coming my way. I was going to have to deal with nearly a dozen deaths of people close to me.

I don't think I ever saw what my cousin was handing me as a threat or a big deal. And I know for sure that she didn't. I think at that age I simply thought it was simply another kind of cigarette. It didn't seem like something that was going to take me down a similar path like my two older brothers who died from overdoses. After their young deaths, I was convinced I would never try heroin because I knew that that was the substance that killed them. But no one told me that it wasn't about the substance but the "addiction brain" behind the substance. No one identified the real villain being genetically passed throughout our family. It just never clicked that even though other substances killed my other family members--all were addicted--addicted to something. Heroin doesn't kill you, addiction to it does. Alcohol doesn't kill you, addiction to it does. Lack of understanding the addiction neurology is what kills. Activating and growing the addiction neurology in yourself is what kills. Gateway substances train our brains to seek outside substances to deal with emotional, physical or psychological pain. Once you get on that train it often doesn't stop--unless you stop it.

"I'm just doing this socially." How many times have you heard that? How many times have you said that? *That innocent little drink. That innocent little hit.* People forget that a tidal wave or Tsunami all starts from one innocuous drop of water too. But as the momentum of the process builds, one drop adds to another, and those two get added to two more, and those four become six, and so on. That one drop that has now multiplied itself has just become a killer. Similarly, that one sip or one hit is not as innocuous as you think. You have no idea what you are doing to yourself. Again, you started "in control" but you ended "out of control." I don't know if you are an addict in training, an addict who is just entering the gateway to hell, or an addicted person who is currently sitting at the bottom of it, but wherever you are, you can still turn this around. You can fight your way back to "control."

And for those of you at the beginning of this slippery slope, let's be honest about a few things: if you are drinking, smoking, or snorting to be accepted by a group, you are not in control. They control you. That one little weakness (the need to be accepted, or that false sense of feeling good) is about to be exploited in a way that you cannot comprehend. In the same way you are letting that group dominate you, that chemical will dominate you. If you think these words are just dramatic talk, you're already inebriated. I speak from the experience of every step of this downward journey. I'm trying to save you. So listen, and save yourself. My professional advice is this: When they sip, snort, puff and then pass to you, pass on it. If they don't want to accept you for exercising a healthier choice for yourself, they are not your friends anyway. If they look down upon you for looking out for your personal well-being, they just demonstrated they truly don't give a damn about you in reality. It's not worth it. And those people are not worth it.

Ally:

Maybe it's too late for your friend or family member. Maybe they are way past the gateway. Maybe they are already on the road of addiction and you're in the thick of things trying to get them to recovery. Perhaps you're the person who innocently offered the addicted person their first use of the drug and now regret it. I wish you luck and send you prayers to get them into recovery. But right now, I want to highlight addiction prevention. We rarely talk about the following aspect of things. So, let me just say it all very plainly.

If you really want to be an ally, **stop passing drinks and drugs to people in social situations.** If they didn't ask for it, don't offer it. And if they do, be hesitant to share it. If you must, offer it with a warning conversation. It could help a person refrain from doing something they know they have no business doing. Just that one thing could help them not fall for the peer pressure they were about to fall right into. Let them know they are still cool with you, accepted, and can be comfortable hanging out without joining the crowd by using--just because everyone else is. Do you know how many lives that one conversation could save? Countless.

The disease of addiction is considered a noncommunicable disease. But that's not true. I say the use and abuse of psychoactive drugs and beverages have such a socialization element to them, the addictions they spawn could be considered "communicably transferred."

This is what happens when you pass a drug to a person with this hereditary condition. You're not doing them a favor. Unbeknownst to you, you could be complicit in ending a life. Every overdose started on one day, in one situation, from one, first, hit. It started with an *introduction*. It started with a gateway.

Clinician:

Sometimes we have to get out of the treatment clinic and into the community to teach. A lot of the clients we see coming through our doors--at the lowest points of their lives--started from social or casual drug use. I think we need to do more to show our communities the real picture of addiction and mental health from the beginning of the road to the end of it. There are people at bars and parties right now ingesting substances having no idea what those chemical reactions can lead to. I'm writing this book right now as a way of getting my knowledge out of the clinic and into the community.

I'm tired of seeing people at the end of the road, decimated. Having the conversations early is called "prevention." We all know knowledge is power, and we need to give people power over this disease before it even starts. I want to get out in front of the problem before it starts. And that *beginning* is the first hit or the first sip. People really and truly think it is harmless. And they have no idea what's coming for them. Yes, we are equipped to treat them, but we are also equipped to teach them. More community outreach NOW. Let's talk about it. Let's have community conversations about mental health and addiction.

Recovery:

If you recognize yourself in the early steps of this road, I advise you to abruptly turn yourself around. All of our addiction calamities started from one drink, one hit. For me, it started with someone as innocent as my babysitter, my beloved cousin. A casual choice can become something serious and sinister. Help is available. Seek it.

RECOVERY PEARL:

"When people say, 'Drink responsibly,' for a lot of you that means, 'Don't drink at all.'"

Chapter 4

Is My Teen Getting High?

"Do parents really want to know?"
- Lucy Hall

CHAPTER 4

Is My Teen Getting High?

The teen years are difficult for child and parent alike. Adding addiction to the mix escalates the situation, turning things volatile quickly. Once a child leaves your home they are exposed to every societal ill, including drugs, addicted peers, and dealers. Without attentive parenting, kids' rebellious experimentations can go very bad. They can even be fatal.

I'm a parent--*a busy one.* I always say parents <u>choose</u> not to know their child is using drugs. I say this because I'm here to keep it real and save lives. Parents know their children. They know the child better than the child knows itself. They've been learning the child longer than the child has been self-aware. They've watched the child's personality and patterns develop from the very beginning. Every little quirk in that child's way of being is known. When something is amiss, parents get the signs. They get the hints. They see subtle changes in behavior. And all too often, when it all goes down-hill, and a situation becomes non-recoverable, parents look back in painful regret and reflection. *"You know, I do remember that one thing, that one day. I just didn't take it seriously. If I would have, maybe things would be different. Maybe my child would be alive today."*

Illustration:

I'm a 30-years clean former addict in recovery for life. I'm an addiction counselor. I'm also CEO of a successful addiction recovery center--all by God's grace. I have high visibility in the community for what I do. Lives have been touched. Lives have been saved. Now, imagine how I felt when my own kid walked into my house high as a kite one day. It was not pretty. I was livid.

My boy was a high schooler at the time. My life transformation had afforded us the opportunity to live in a great neighborhood. It also afforded my son the opportunity to attend the best schools that my area had to offer. During that time, like most teens, my son was dealing with a socialization issue--looking for groups to fit in with--learning how to form social bonds. It's just part of the way kids grow up. But here's the thing: My son is an African-American male with a mother who fought to recover herself from the grips of addiction death. We were one of those bottom to the top American stories. God raised me out of hell into a sober, successful business life. My son was attending a high school where the socio-economic population was very different from him. His school was very rich and very white. He was neither. But he still had to figure out how to fit in.

My son used to hang out with two kids named Jay and P.K. from school. *Boy oh boy, these two*. I thought I'd done everything I could to ensure my kid would never fall into the same traps and trips that I did growing up. I wanted the Hall clan to have a brand new start. The legacy of addiction and premature death was going to stop with me--as far as I was concerned. That sound naive? You bet it does.

My son and his buddy Jay were *hanging out* at my house one day. They were in the backyard and I was in the kitchen cooking dinner. They were far away from the back windows, down by the lake. I did not know what the two boys were up to. But by the time I called them in to have dinner, it was clear. I yelled out, "Dinner's ready! Come inside!" With God as my witness, my son entered my house looking just "dumb" in the face. Something was dragging the appearance of his face like his IQ had just dropped 20 points. He was curiously nervous and kind of crazy acting. I looked closer at his face and I noticed something. His eyes were kind of glassy. I then looked further and it hit me. Oh my God! Not this! Not here! Not now! Not HIM!

I could not believe that I was seeing what I was seeing. In that moment, I certainly could have chosen to blow it off and ignore it. I could have chosen to let that moment pass, acting like I did not see what I just saw. But, *hell no.* I had lost too many family members to this damned disease. I hit the roof with complete anger. I told his little weed-head friend to leave my house. And--*oh boy*--I went off on my son in a way he probably never knew was legally permissible for a mother to do. That boy had it coming and I gave it all to him with no filter. When his friend closed the door, I hit my boy upside his head like he was in a serious street squabble. I cursed him something fierce. He was like, *"Ma! Ma!"* He was high and trying to calm me down. But, *no.* I completely ruined his high. By the time we finished going back and forth, heatedly arguing, he ran away to his room and closed the door. I didn't care. My perspective was this: The boy should be glad he was still alive--because if drugs didn't take him out, I surely was.

The next day the emotions had finally calmed. I went into my son's room. I sat on the edge of his bed. We talked. We had a heart to heart. We had an in-depth conversation about addiction. I had to tell him my story. And of course my kids are always like, "Mom! C'mon! I'm not gonna do that!" And I'm forever looking at them skeptically, like, "Ok. All I know is you now have knowledge. Use it wisely."

That blow-up episode and that talk slowed him down. I don't think he smoked quite a long while after that. He's now grown and living on the West Coast where it's legal now; I just found out he's smoking marijuana again. Oh well. He's an adult now. All I can do is pray fervently--pray it does not escalate, triggering the addiction neurology he may have inherited genetically. I pray it does not become his gateway to a slow and dangerous decline. My duty as his mom is to educate, pray, and always leave the door of communication open.

These kids will try anything at anytime. They have no idea. We must give them understanding, and firmly. My teenage son and his little high-as-a-kite friend were supremely checked on that day. Today my adult son swears to me he only uses marijuana sparingly for medical purposes. He says it's a painkilling treatment to help with a longtime sports injury, as well as his anxiety. He tells me he's not abusing at all and not interested in doing so.

Unfortunately, things did not go as well for his friend P.K. The two remained friends into their young adult years. However, about two weeks ago we attended his funeral. P.K. died of a heroin overdose. May he rest in peace.

Addict:

Two of my brothers experimented with drugs in their teens. Both are dead. The youngest died three days before his high-school graduation. When my eldest died, they found him dead on the bathroom floor, overdosed on heroin. I remember everyone crying, completely devastated to see a child dead. I remember these events vividly.

The death of my two brothers left me wounded. It scarred me deeply. It scared the hell out of me. And though I knew drug use was killing member after member of my family, drug use was the only thing that took the edge off of dealing with the pain of their deaths. I was caught in the perfect trap. And trapped I was.

I was a teen. I became a young weed head. In a sick and twisted way, I was glad to be one. I was better. I was safe. Weed wasn't the demon of alcohol which took my mother, nor the heroin needles that killed my two brothers in the prime of their lives. So by the time smoking cocaine came around as a thing in the 80's, I equally considered cocaine way better than what my mother and brothers were doing. Amazing to imagine that kind of logic, right? Sounds crazy and it absolutely was. I had personal drug-use ethics and I was strongly convicted about them. I knew I didn't want to drink myself to death and was vehemently against shooting needles into my arm. Self-righteously, I would have none of that. I was above that. And simultaneously, I was smoking crack? See how the mind of an addict works? A mind on drugs is cunning, dangerous and stupid. Weed was my gateway. It got me used to reaching for substances to medicate my emotions. If who I was reminds you of who you are, seek recovery now before it's too late. I barely made it out. So many do not.

Ally:

Again, I'm a parent. I know how hard the job is. I am never here to judge. I can't. I know how unpredictable kids can be--especially teens. It's impossible to watch them 24/7. But we can certainly watch for the signs.

According to some reports, 34.9% of 12th grade students have reported using marijuana in the last year and 21.3% have used in the last 30 days. Some reports say nearly 50% of teenagers admit to misusing a prescription or illicit substance at least one time in their brief lives. That's what teens are reportedly telling us outright. Imagine all of what they are not saying. Did *you* tell the whole truth as a teen?

As parents we must go the extra mile; if we love our children, we must. When I discovered my son Christian was up to something, as a hands-on mother and busy career woman I did not need one more thing to deal with. But I had to. And I did. There's no denying when someone has just encountered a mind or mood altering drug. On cocaine you can't stay still. On alcohol you slur. On heroin you're nodding out. And on marijuana you're ravenously hungry, your eyes are glassy, and all of them make you look dumb in the face. How do you not confront that, whether it's your child, your mate, your coworker? Have the conversation! Don't you be in denial too!

"If you love me, confront me." That's the unsaid motto of every addict in trouble or on the road to trouble. You must confront what is looking at you. If you know your child, you know good and well something is off. You should question their behavior. Do not be afraid to ask the right questions. I will always challenge young people to examine themselves and their motives. Again, knowledge is power.

Until this very day, my daughter claims I went soft when it came to Christian. I admit--I did. I let my guard down with him. Here I was out in a good suburban neighborhood thinking my family was going to be free of all the risks.

My son was attending a good school, surrounded by students who were pretty well-off. And sometimes that is the very problem. Students with a lot of money (or access to a lot of money) have the means to get themselves into a lot of mischief. My son was a minority at a rich white school. He wanted to fit in. He wanted to be accepted by his rich friends. So he did what kids do--follow the group. They do everything to "fit in." And to my naive surprise, that included smoking and drinking.

Admittedly, I bought into the hype. I fell prey to the stereotypes. Something in me foolishly thought my child would not be turned on to drugs because he was going to a private school in the suburbs. Clearly, that was not the case. These kids were also into everything. Maybe more. And everything and anything was easily obtained for them.

I began letting my son spend the night over these friends' houses without properly vetting their families. And that was a mistake on my part. I was being naive and slack as a parent. And that's *shame on me.* Even I fell asleep at the wheel. I should have known way, way, way better as CEO of Mary Hall Freedom House. *Why?* Because we treat people from every racial, national and socio-economic background at my facility--people most would never expect. I tell you, stereotypes are a terrible thing. I couldn't believe I fell for it. In my judgement, drugs are as pervasive and rampant in the rich communities as in the hood. There is just more money to make it look otherwise.

Rich or poor, our children have access to every illicit substance today. But what they need more access to is "us." More parental presence in our children's lives can make a world of difference. We need to halt our busy lives and spend more quality one-on-one time with our children. If you're a parent, take note of everything I've said here and stay woke. Stay vigilant. And most of all, stay emotionally "connected" with your child. Don't let them face the temptations of this world alone. Presence matters.

Clinician:

"Our work" is bigger than "our job." We get to save lives. But we also get to save families if we take the initiative. When counseling clients, it's advised to ask about their children--especially their teens. Explain that this is a hereditary disease. You may be surprised how many people do not get that. When children enter the teen and/or pre-teen years, they start to deal with complex emotions they may not be equipped to handle--like loneliness and social pressures and manipulations from the wrong crowd. They often turn to drugs or alcohol to help them cope with what they are afraid to tell their parents.

The previous applies to all teens, but imagine how much more it applies to children of addicts. They are likely in more distress, dealing with an extremely broken home life, plus dealing with a genetic predisposition. Go back and read the chapter which talks about why we use in the first place. If you understand what is being said there, you will understand why children of addicts (in particular) are so at risk. And not just that, children of addicts are more likely to role model the addiction behavior of their parents. It's not always a conscious choice. So when bringing recovery treatment to a client, focus on healing that client, but also bring their family (and especially their children) into the healing conversation. Otherwise, this cycle simply repeats. All too often, addiction can become a family affair.

To Recovery:

Parents of teens, be mindful. Parents of teens who have addiction in their families, be extra mindful. I met my son's father while in an A.A. meeting. We were recovering together. My daughter's father was the one who introduced me to crack cocaine. Both of my children have the genetic threat on both sides. I was hyper-alert about their welfare when they were teens. Now that they are adults, I keep them armed with information. I will keep my eyes on them until my dying day. It's a parent's job. If you see changes in your teen, get proactive. Take control of the situation. Don't be so busy trying to be a friend to your children that you forget to be a parent. And if there is a problem, seek recovery support right away. There's no debate. Force them if you have to; have those conversations that hurt but are necessary. Do so with vigilance, guidance and compassion. It's your job, my job, our job. Save these children.

RECOVERY PEARL:

"Teens experiment, but teens of addicts cannot afford to."

Chapter 5

How to Survive an Overdose

"Addiction is always a life and death matter."
- Lucy Hall

CHAPTER 5

How to Survive an Overdose

By age thirteen *"five"* of my close family members had died from alcohol related death or drug overdose. *Did you hear what I just said?* Two of my brothers overdosed on heroin; my aunt overdosed on alcohol; my grand-mother passed from alcohol, and my beloved mother both died from alco-holism. I lost my mother when I was only 6 years of age. For a little over a decade I watched addiction chop down my family tree. Addiction was a real, living, breathing demon eating us away person by person. Why would I be surprised when it finally turned its appetites upon me? In retrospect, it was inevitable. I was young when it started. I was barely an adolescent. It was my turn to die. I began my own slow march toward the grave. And at that point--in my young mind--early death was just what life was about. I could feel it coming.

Illustration:

Overdose and early death is the end of the road for an addicted person's life--just like any other chronic disease. It's real. Every time I see it happen to a person, I think: *that's me in the life that would have been.* Recently I witnessed another overdose story play out. It was truly heartbreaking. It happened to a young girl I knew. I watched her mother go through one of the most painful things a mother could ever go through--and we all know what that is.

One day I received a frantic call from the mother. She told me she'd just received a cryptic text from her daughter's phone. It was very odd and unlike her, not to mention something was amiss with the Google app the text was sent from. The mom didn't get the message until days after it was sent. The whole situation just wasn't right.

I could hear in the tone of her voice that she suspected the worst. Her daughter was a recovering addict who had gotten herself clean for quite some time. The mother thought it was possible her daughter was back out there using. All of her inner-alarms were going off. And by the time we talked the daughter had been missing for days. There was nothing I could do. We both suspected relapse was the issue.

I offered to pray with the mother. She accepted. We did. She then asked me to call the daughter's phone. I did. I left the daughter a voicemail letting her know she was always welcome to come to Mary Hall Freedom House and get it all straightened out again. I wanted her to know that I was here to help her get back on the road to recovery. I told her there was always a space for her. Sadly, I don't think she ever received that message. The mom received the cryptic text that Monday, called me on Tuesday, and the daughter's body was found on Friday. She had overdosed. She was gone. It was devastating.

Reportedly the young lady went to what is commonly known here in Atlanta as "The Bluff." It can be a perfect place to go on a destructive drug binge. And it's where she relapsed. And it's where she died. "The Bluff" took her dead, overdosed body and put it in the nearby park where she was finally found. Earlier in the week they said a guy who knew her got out in the streets searching for her until he came across her body discarded in that park. Ironically, he was a guy she had helped to get clean.

Addict:

Unfortunately this young lady's story is not rare. She relapsed as too many do. She walked away from her new recovery lifestyle. I don't know what triggered that, but something did--and it had fatal consequences. No parent should have to bury a child. My prayers go out to her mother and father. I am so saddened that their child had to die from this ridiculous disease.

Too many relapsing addicts think they can just start shooting-up where they left off, and that's not true. If you turn away from recovery you can't go back to using the substance at the same level of dosage you did before you got clean. If you do, you put yourself in deadly danger. Your body just cannot take that. Once you get clean, those amounts are a shock to the system. Plus, people unknowingly mix all kinds of substances to get high--not knowing they are creating deadly combinations of chemicals. I've seen this too many times and cannot say it enough. If you have been using for five or ten years, and you get clean from heroin for three years, then relapse, you cannot shoot the same quantity of heroin into your veins as you did before; you could explode your heart. If you are a heroin user or are addicted to opioid painkillers, you should always carry an Opioid Overdose Prevention Toolkit. Go to SAMHSA.gov. Search: "Opioid Overdose Prevention Toolkit." Download yours today. Protect yourself. There are critical tools available that can reverse an overdose until help arrives. Read below.

Ally:

Reports say over 100 people die from opioid overdose per day--a figure that is rapidly rising. Because of the spike in opioid use today (Heroin, Prescription Painkillers, Fentanyl), there are anti-overdose medications that addicted people can use these days to help stop an overdose and prevent death. Some carry the *Envizio* device which injects the drug Naloxone into the body. It helps counteract an overdose when it's happening. This drug can help an overdosing addict start breathing again--at least for a while, until help arrives. But you must call 911 once the overdose starts because there is only a brief window of time that the Naloxone holds back the effect of the overdose. After that window, the person will stop breathing again. There is also a nasal sprayer on the market called *Narcan*. It delivers Naloxone into the system as well by releasing it into one nostril.

Devices like these are helping to save lives during this epidemic. As an ally, a friend or loved one of a heroin abuser (or any other kind of opioid), it is STRONGLY advised that you keep these overdose prevention devices on you at all times. Have your addicted loved ones carry a supply as well. Educate yourselves on the proper use of these tools. During overdose, they buy critical time until an ambulance arrives. Since their availability on the market, thousands of lives have been saved by non-professionals. Be proactive. What you know or don't know (have or don't have) can make the difference in your loved one's life or death. Get an Opioid Overdose Prevention Toolkit. Go to SAMHSA.gov. Search: Opioid Overdose Prevention Toolkit. Download today.

Clinician:

As clinicians and facility owners we have to do more to educate our communities about opioid overdose prevention. Far too many people still do not know that tools like *Narcan* and *Envizio* are available. Addiction in our communities is real and we need to do all we can. Community organizations that care to do something can have café conversations and "friend-raisers" to do mass purchases and distribute these tools widely. Every little bit helps to reduce the death rates due to overdose. Statistics are already showing that communities which have Naloxone (*Narcan & Envizio)* in wide distribution are seeing sharp declines in overdose deaths. Let's bring this disease from the shadows and make it front-and-center in the community discussion. Let's do what we can to save real lives now. Educate and distribute.

To Recovery:

I'm so glad to know there are things out there that will help resuscitate people during overdose. Social policies and community tools like this are huge steps in right direction. It shows a developing maturity when it comes to how we approach the addiction problem as a society. I also applaud the non-punitive laws like the Good Samaritan Laws which are active in many states. They allow bystanders, family members and others "legal immunity" when they call for help if they witness an overdose in progress. Our society might be slowly realizing addiction is actually a ***DISEASE***--worthy of ***medical help***--not a crime deserving punishment.

Sadly, the opioid epidemic our country is experiencing right now is going to take a lot of lives before things get better. Let's double down on our efforts and help people get educated and better prepared to prevent overdoses. If you are suffering from an addiction to opiates or any other addiction, there is a way out other than the grave. Find a highly reputable recovery center or a recovery community organization in your area. Beat the statistics.

RECOVERY PEARL:

"The best way to survive an overdose is to not use."

Chapter 6

When Addiction Turns Violent or Criminal

"In the depths of this disease, people will do anything to get that next high."
- Lucy Hall

CHAPTER 6

When Addiction Turns Violent or Criminal

In the addict's mind, everything is prioritized beneath the thirst to use. Nothing is more important than getting high--and whatever they have to do to get to that high. That might include theft. That might include violence. That might include prostitution. That might include abandoning children. And it definitely includes self-destruction. When push comes to shove, don't think an addicted mind will not include you in their destructive fall. Desperation to get high creates desperate acts. Trust me, I know what I'm speaking of.

Illustration:

I'm almost ashamed to speak on it. Addiction took me so low that I resorted to crime as a means to support my habit. The disease made me conniving, diabolical and clever about it. I became a bonafide thief to get the money I needed for drugs. I was chasing the next high and was going to get it by any means necessary. Stealing from department stores became the crime of choice to pay for my drug of choice. I was young, out of control and very addicted to *crack cocaine.*

I was never the kind who walks into a store and starts outright stealing. I had sense enough to know that would not go well, resulting in me being caught quickly and prevented from getting high. That was not going to work. This needed to be successful. So, I started stealing in a smart way--if there is any way in hell that you can call stealing "smart."

I remember a cousin of mine would go into department stores to do basic shoplifting. She'd enter a dressing room, slip on a new pair of jeans under the ones she wore into the store, and just walk out. I thought she was crazy and would soon get caught.

One day she urged me to try it. She wanted me to do the exact same thing. But as I mentioned, I thought it was basic and dumb. Then--stupidly--I did it. I entered a dressing room. I slipped on some new and expensive jeans beneath my old ones. As soon as I tried to walk out like I'd seen her do--*boom*--I was caught. *Damn. I knew it!*

But I was so lucky that time! The owner of the store in Tuckahoe, NY could see that I was a first time rookie doing something I already knew I had no business doing--and could not do well. My nervousness surely gave me away. That store owner had mercy on me. He made me march back into that dressing room, take the jeans off, and put them back. He sent me away with a warning. But did I learn my lesson that day? Yes, I did. I learned I could not do my cousin's kind of stupid stealing. My addicted brain started working. I still needed to get that high! Any sane person would have walked away and left the criminal activity to the criminals. But this disease removes that kind of sensible logic. I needed a solution--a way to get the drugs. My little brain started thinking and scheming.

Eventually, I landed on an idea. I majorly upgraded my thievery--coming up with an entirely different way to fleece Macy's and every department store who let me into their doors. And I did so without detection. Sadly, my new technique worked flawlessly. I had figured out a way to walk into any fancy downtown department store, with nothing, and walk right back out the door with (sometimes) hundreds of dollars in cold, hard, cash in my hand. Worse, I could wave at the security guard on my way out without a problem. He might even open the door for me. I stole untold sums of money--with a heist crew of one--a very addicted and twisted crew of one. I was so sick in the head. I actually thought myself to be some kind of *sophisticated* thief. But isn't a thief just a damned thief?

Eventually, that wasn't enough. I started searching out specific retail jobs which would put me near the money. I loved being a cashier. I invented seamless schemes to skim money from employers on top of my weekly paycheck. *Why?* Because a paycheck wasn't enough money--it could be smoked in one hour. Things got so bad that I landed a job as a bank teller, overseeing mail-deposits. Listen to me. It was my job to open envelopes full of cash, to count the cash, and sort it all out. *Uh-oh. Why in the world did they hire me for that?*

I remember my first day, vividly. I sat there opening all of those envelopes. There was cash on top of cash right before my eyes--the eyes of a crack-cocaine addict. It made me a nervous wreck because stealing this cash would be bonafide bank robbery--a federal crime--with federal time. Four hours into that dang job and I was just shaking. I could not trust myself. When they called for lunchtime, I got up, collected my things, then walked right out of that bank and never went back. They could keep that half-a-day's paycheck. I just wanted to be away from all that federal offense cash. That bank was not the place for my addicted self. I had to go back to my regular department store schemes. Because it just worked. And I needed it to keep working.

I took up all kinds of small thieving. I would steal my father's credit cards and hang out at the gas station with my cousin. We'd walk up to people saying, "Hey let me fill up your tank on this card. Just give me that $20 (or more) in cash." People would go for it every time because it was a win-win. They'd get more gas and we'd get cold cash. Dealers didn't take credit cards. But my appetite for cocaine kept growing. It wasn't enough. That's the way addiction is; it's about more, more, and more.

After being so successful at my Lord & Taylor's department store heist for so long, I tried to pull off the same crime at another regional department store--similar to a K-Mart. And that's when the wheels fell off. That's when they caught me.

I was trying to do my same little scheme on bigger ticket items for more cash. What else could I do? I wasn't going to go back to the bank. I needed larger amounts of the drug to get me to the high I needed to get to. So I walked into that department store, young, confident, sick, and a fool. Those people watched every step of my so-called sophisticated scheme from the front door, to the aisle, and back again. I was fooling no one but myself. The next thing I know, two men were slapping handcuffs on me and shoving me into the back of a police car. I WAS SO SCARED! It was probably the worst and best day of my young adult life. I cried so hard in that backseat that those cops decided to take the cuffs off of me. And that was probably symbolic. Because little did I know God was about to free my addicted soul for the very first time in my life. It was that very arrest which ushered me into the life of recovery I lead today. It put me on the road to treatment, health and sanity again.

Addict:

The disease of addiction is ruthless. It will turn people who have the disease into ruthless individuals doing ruthless things. It will turn you against the people you love. It will turn you against your community. When in active addiction, we live to use and use to live. Nothing has more priority than the next high. Some of you who are currently suffering with the addicted brain listened to my story, sifting it for tips on how to get quick cash to pay for your habit. I know how you think because I used to be you. I thought in the same diseased way. This condition removes all shame. Notice how I talked about the department store stealing without ever describing what I did? There is a reason. I know addicts are in my audience.

I remember in my early days of recovery, not long after I got clean, I was confessing every little crazy, nefarious thing I did to get high. I was purging my soul. But I finally realized that sometimes I was simply helping the sick get sicker--and--slicker. One day I told another girl in recovery my Lord and Taylor's thieving story. I told it in explicit detail, the whole technique. I thought I was showing her how low I had fallen and inspiring her to do better than me. I was encouraging her on the recovery journey to fly straight. Then I saw what was really going on.

One day I went with her to the department store to shop. We were both in recovery now. And I could not believe my eyes. I saw this woman take the technique I shared and do exactly what she learned from me--right in front of me--it scared the hell out of me. Here I was clean and sober, thinking I had left that life far behind, and here she was repeating it. That woke me up. I wanted nothing more to do with that life, and could not afford to be around it or people who were committed to living it. It was insanity. From that day on, I stopped giving that testimony--not in that level of detail. I had forgotten I was talking to the addicted mind.

Isn't it sad what this disease can make us do? And the destructive brilliance it can inspire? We hurt so many people while under the influence. We do so many unspeakable things. I sent my own father through pure hell. And he was such a good man--a very good man. He did not deserve what I put him through. But I did. The man had already been through enough, losing his wife to alcohol addiction, losing his sons to overdoses, then trying to raise the rest of us without my mom. And, how did I thank him? I grew up to serve him more hell. Plus, I got pregnant and brought a baby into all my addicted madness--an infant child he would later have to care for while I was away in recovery. So, my question is this: At what point do we stop thinking about ourselves and the next high and seek help? It is true that this is a disease of compulsion, but at what point will we stop and get help for it? At what point do we restore sanity and peace not only to our lives but everyone who loves us? How much pain must we cause to self and others before we reach out for help? When we let this disease fester it's not just our lives circling the drain, it's the lives of everyone we're connected to: children, parents, spouses, friends--even society. Recovery helps us reverse all of this.

Ally:

Addicted neurology can lead to all kinds of personality pathologies. Don't be surprised or caught flat-footed when it strikes. Be aware. Get educated on what is happening to your loved one; know what you are dealing with. Psychoactive substances impair the judgment of dependents. It can completely rearrange their moral or value systems. When this disease is full-throttle, the person you knew and loved is not really there. A distorted version of them is.

Though you see yourself as a helpful ally to an addict, their addicted brain may make them see you as an obstacle, not a person. Don't take that personally. It's just how you are going to be seen through diseased eyes. This disease does so much damage to the cognition of the individual that they no longer think and function like you and I--so don't expect them to. Respect the power of this disease and the possibilities it can bring about. The addicted brain often considers family members, loved ones or friends to be intrusive hinderances to their explosive addiction cravings. To some people in active addiction even their little children are nuisances to their addiction needs. Some will steal from children, parents and grandparents to get a hit. Translation: You are a target. It does not matter how much you love them. If you truly understand that this is a neurologically based disease, you understand these are not choices of character. It is a neurological/physiological compulsion. Root yourself in this understanding so that you will not take transgressions against you personally and still be able to be the ally they need to help them eventually get out of this condition. But while providing this help, there is a deep need to be aware and position yourself for any possibility.

My advice? Do not leave temptations around the addicted. If you see their loss of personal control deepening--and there is the threat of danger, loss of morality, criminal activity or violence--have contingency plans. Be prepared. Protect yourself, vulnerable family members, your property and your valuables. If you find yourself or your loved ones fearing for your lives or safety at any time, you will have to involve law enforcement. Explain the situation, the addiction and the fact that it is a loved one to the dispatch caller, so the authorities will treat the situation as a medical one and not a criminal one. It is a ruthless disease; it can turn a person you love into a ruthless individual.

Clinician:

At Mary Hall Freedom House, we keep discipline and order with compassion. As professionals, we already know that safeguarding our sessions and facility is a real thing. Well-planned precaution and persistent vigilance is always necessary when dealing with this disease. However, with that being said, addicts and alcoholics are addicts and alcoholics. And they do what addicts and alcoholics do. At Mary Hall Freedom House, we know this. And because we know this, we will never put a person out simply based on their disease. That seems counterproductive to us. We don't punish or criminalize the disease itself. Can you see a medical practitioner penalizing a cancer patient for a cancer relapse, or punishing a bipolar person for having a bi-polar episode? It just doesn't make sense. We are here to **TREAT** the condition, not penalize it.

It is a firm and compassionate balancing act. We certainly have strict policies and we strongly enforce them to keep clients, visitors and workers safe. But the process is a lot more nuanced than that. We even turn relapses into powerful teaching moments for people in recovery. We aim to use those instances of "bottoming-out" as catalysts to go deeper into the recovery and healing process. However, if a person exercises their disease while attempting to take someone else in the program down with them, to use with them, or put some other attendee in jeopardy in a different or similar way, that is grounds for a swift expulsion from our program. And for sure--addicted or not--criminality or violence is a line we do not allow our clients to cross. We have a NO TOLERANCE POLICY. If crossed, expulsion is immediate. But if a client has a breakdown only causing harm to self (barring outright drug use on our properties) we can start over with the person in need. Again, we are not here to punish addiction behavior, we are here to treat it. Yet, there are limits.

To Recovery:

I don't know what you have done while under the influence--but you do. This disease can turn you into things you never imagined you could be. Don't put your family, loved ones or innocent society members at risk, harm or danger. Get help. Seek your nearest recovery center, recovery community organization or 12-Step Meeting. Do this for all involved. Restore your dignity. I did it. You can too. All of this is reversible--and NOW.

RECOVERY PEARL:

"Victims of this disease eventually victimize others for the next high."

Chapter 7

I Gotta Hit Rock-Bottom?

"Many go way down, but only some come back up."
— Lucy Hall

CHAPTER 7

I Gotta Hit Rock-Bottom?

Bottom is a powerful catalyst to change. It either turns your life around or out-and-out kills you. The *hope* here is that an addict voluntarily chooses a pathway to that change before losing the option. *Bottom* takes away all options. The typical life of addiction is just one long spin-out before one huge wipe-out. By the time it all goes over the cliffs, many lives can wind up totaled beyond repair (the life of the addict, lives of family members, lives of friends). *Rock-bottom* is when you've fallen so low you cannot fall any further. Most think an addict cannot fall any lower than the grave--they can. When an addict drags a child or mate (or innocent stranger) into the pit of hell with them, it can feel lower than the grave itself. Think of the drunk driver who kills an entire family by accident, but lives to suffer and commiserate about it. That could be a never ending bottom. My eternal advice: break your fall before your bottom does.

Illustration:

I finally woke up to the fact that I had a problem when I was being read my Miranda Rights. My epiphany happened as I was being cuffed and hauled away. It was like a holy moment in an unholy place and an unholy situation. My whole life was about to change. Sitting in the back of a squad car like a caught animal is when I knew something had gone terribly wrong in my life. I was never the kind of person who was built for jail or having my freedom taken from me. Languishing in the back of that car, I wondered, *How in the hell did I end up here?* It was a sobering moment. Sometimes people need that--*a sobering moment.*

My addiction had taken me so far down that I had resorted to petty stealing in the stores. I was "boosting," as they say. And I was "busted," as they also say. I had to come home and tell my dad about what happened and what they did to me. That was excruciating for me. That man did not deserve that. I had just had a baby. I had been sending him through hell, trying to help me. Looking back, it was that moment that started my wake-up process. Being hauled off to jail was rock-bottom for me. Ultimately, it is what made me determined to change. I didn't want my daughter to grow up not having a mother. I'd lived that life.

Addict:

Every addict's bottom is different. Some come within an inch of death during overdose. Some accidentally kill someone else. Some permanently lose their children or marriage. Some lose their freedom with a lengthy prison sentence. Some even contract a deadly disease. It can be anything. It was the potential loss of my freedom that turned me around. My question is this: What has to happen to you to turn you around from your binge of destruction? Rock-bottom is a painful experience--an experience you do not have to go through before change. It is actually possible to change from choice instead of force. It is possible to change before death.

When nearing rock-bottom, it is no longer a secret that you're an addict. You know, your family knows, the world knows. It's not about being oblivious to your condition at this point. It's no longer about embarrassment. It's about *"if not now, when?"* You know this speeding train of destruction is headed for a cliff, but you've been lucky so far. You've been cheating fate. You've been gambling with your chances. And you know how gambling goes; you can win and win and until you LOSE BIG--until you lose it all. I'm talking about your life. Why wait that long? Why let things go that far if you know you have a problem that can be dealt with? Remember: You're never alone dealing with this disease. Millions are dealing with it. Be of the responsible few willing to courageously get help before hitting a bottom you can never recover from.

Ally:

A lot of times we're only "so-called allies" of the addicted people in our lives. Often, we are silent enablers. But what will we do on the day the addict dies and their blood is on our hands? How can we live with their deaths forever stained on our conscience? Silently enabling is not being an ally. That's not helping a person prevent rock-bottom. That's just watching them plummet until they go "splat" all over the jagged rocks.

After decades in this work, I've seen it all. I've seen all kinds of enablers trying to *make nice* about nasty things. I've seen mothers actually buy drugs for their addicted children--thinking they're helping the child avoid further risk by buying the drugs from a drug-dealer for the child. I've seen celebrity addicts aided by an army of enablers--the "yes men" and "yes women"--on the payroll of a person who is clearly very sick. Not interceding before a person hits their rock-bottom could be considered as serious as aiding and abetting a death. It's like assisting a slow suicide. Trust me, I've seen every case. It all makes sense to a *"yes man"* and *"yes woman"* until the celebrity dies. Afterwards, all the close aides are dragged into the media, questioned and scrutinized for never saying anything--or worse--helping the celebrity to get the drugs.

Being a true ally is about telling the person you care about, exactly what they *need* to hear, versus what they *want* to hear--PERIOD. It's about helping to save a person's life when they have lost the clarity to save their own. Intervene before you've lost the opportunity to. If you're a "yes man" or "yes woman," afraid of losing your job, let me ask you something: *Isn't your job still lost once the powerful person is dead from overdose?* You have a better chance of retaining your relationship and employment if the powerful person is alive and healthy. Don't you think so?

Clinician:

When an addict survives rock-bottom, they finally come see us to pick up all the broken pieces. But some clients may have more breaking to do. If you run a facility in a large city anything like ours, you will one day have to treat a rich or famous person--or--a lot of them. Often, wealth and/or fame is an entirely separate intoxicant to deal with--on top of the chemicals already flowing through a powerful addict's bloodstream. It's a deadly mix. For a lot of these people, just being in a facility "is" their rock-bottom. It's so embarrassing for them. It is decimating to their pride. You have to learn how to treat them like any other person with a disease--who is sick, and in need of help. That's exactly what they are--any other person in need. Never get affected by a person's social position and let that prevent you from doing your job effectively. Don't get taken in by their power or fame. Get these people the true help they need. Stay sober minded and help them turn their lives around. Be soft when they need it. Be firm when they need it. Be what they need to get strong in recovery. They need someone who can keep it real with them. You might be the only one in their lives doing so.

Recovery:

I was an intelligent woman, smoking crack. Sounds oxymoronic? It is, but it's not. There are more of us than you think, not just the famous black mayor of Washington, D.C. (Mayor Marion Barry), or the famous crack smoking white mayor of the highly cosmopolitan city, Toronto, Canada (Mayor Rob Ford). Check all of your recent headlines. Addiction is everywhere. It is amidst the highly positioned in life and the lowly positioned in life. It is beyond every stereotype you know. It's just that some people have more money to secretly get it and secretly hide it than others--and that's unfortunate for them. It takes them the longest to fall and hit rock bottom from their high perches in life. It takes them the longest to wake up. If you are one of the highly positioned in your society, and see yourself reflected in these words, seek recovery now. Save your life. Protect your legacy. Help is available.

RECOVERY PEARL:

"Break your fall before the bottom breaks you."

Chapter 8

How to Stage a Successful Intervention

"I love you. And this is what I see."
- Lucy Hall

CHAPTER 8

How to Stage a Successful Intervention

Your loved one is using. They've taken all the money and smoked it up, snorted it up, gambled it up, or sexed it up. If it's your child, they're now likely doing all manner of foolishness in the streets, hanging with foolish people, and possibly bringing foolishness into your home--your sanctuary.

When addiction strikes a household, the air can get tense. The very place built to bring you comfort and shelter from the world now brings you discomfort, threat, and a rising fear. There's an elephant in the room. It needs to be dealt with. It's the disease of addiction.

Remember: Love is "saying something."

Illustration:

There's a lot to be said on how to properly intervene on a person's addiction spiral. Sometimes you get through to them. Sometimes you just don't. Sometimes you plant a powerful seed of reflection into their minds--one that takes root later.

Often the most successfully staged interventions come not from a family member or friend, but from life itself. It comes from what and whom some call God. The creator of your life knows just where to hit you and how to hit you--to get your attention. This happened for one of the ladies in our program. I don't know how many people tried to intervene on her disease before, but when this intervention hit, it hit home.

Stephanie was not unlike many who come through our doors. She had gone through all kinds of horrible dramas in her life. She spiraled out of control in her teen years, falling into a myriad of destructive behaviors. She was abusing all kinds of substances trying to cope with her traumas. She was in and out of jail, bad relationships, street life, a broken home life. She eventually found herself *living to use and using to live.* It's the pit we all fall into with this disease.

Like many, she hit many bottoms but none made her wake up--at least--until the last one. One day Stephanie woke up to the news that one of her closest friends was dead. It was a girl she would regularly hang out with and get high with; the two would always use drugs together. And now, she was dead from an overdose. Naturally, this shook Stephanie to the core. She was shell-shocked and could barely believe the girl was gone. The two had just been together, getting high. And when Stephanie later got the news, she was right in the process of getting high again. Think about that. She was ingesting drugs when she received the news about her friend's death from drugs. For normal people, that would make them put down the drug immediately. For the normal addict, that would make them up the dosage to blunt the pain.

However, the moment certainly grabbed Stephanie in a way that nothing else could up to that point. She became crystal clear that she did not want to die like that. Both girls were using and addicted to the exact same substances to get high. She knew she could have been right next to her friend when she overdosed and died. She knew she could have been the one dead instead--or both could be dead together. Reality was crashing in.

Word got out into the community that Stephanie was shook-up about the death and wanted to change. The mother of the girl who died of overdose heard. She turned away from her grief and sprung into action. She found Stephanie and they had a very deep and emotional conversation, I'm sure. And Stephane was basically tossed into the grieving mother's vehicle and sped from South Carolina to Georgia--to our recovery facility. Stephanie says she had no idea exactly where she was being taken or even the name of our center. She said being in the car with her mother's friend was extremely difficult. I can only imagine the tension. The woman had just buried her daughter and now was doing all she could to prevent another young woman (her daughter's age) from dying too. Stephanie tearfully recalled the grieving mother whisking her to recovery saying, *"My daughter passed away. And some of us have to die for some of us to live! If I can help save someone else's daughter's life I will!"*

Those words still make me emotional at this moment. It was one of the most powerful stories of intervention I had heard in all of my 30 years of recovery. I consider it a "God staged" intervention. I don't know why God chooses some to live and some to die. God chose me out of my family clan. Stephanie seemed chosen to live. Stephanie still keeps the obituary of her friend in her apartment. It's a powerful reminder. *You don't have to live this way. You don't have to die this way.*

Addict:

If you allow yourself to slip deeper and deeper into this condition, you will undoubtedly be confronted by people who love you. What perhaps started as a "private" and personal binge of self-destruction, eventually starts spilling out onto others around you. Your choices will begin to affect loved ones, friends, co-workers. They will all notice you're losing control and falling apart--especially when you don't. Your subtle changes of behavior will alert them that something is wrong. They suspect you are using, abusing and headed to a really bad place. And because they love you, they will try to intercede, interrupt, and intervene. They will try to save you from yourself and the grips of a brutal disease that is having its way with you. Expect it. If you were them, would you not do the same thing for the people you love?

Here's what's key to remember: You're the only one in denial about your condition. And, yes, you will most certainly be emotionally triggered by their attempts to help you. You will take it personally, like an attack on your character. But all in all, know that it is love. They see you drowning and they have stopped their own lives to reach into that swirling dark water that is now your life--to pull you out. They did not have to do that, beloved. They do not have to do that. They don't owe you that. And though you may feel highly angered and annoyed that someone else is barging into your personal domain and personal business, you need to focus on their motivations. These people do not desire to be in any difficult emotional entanglement with you. Who wants that? They want to help, even if you are too twisted in mind (right now) to know you need that help. Did you get that? These are people trying to love you.

After they confront you, after they leave, in the next moment of private reflection, the following is what you want to courageously say to yourself.

SELF-REFLECTIONS AFTER INTERVENTION

1. You know what? Maybe I do need to take a look at this.

2. How am I going to address this?

3. What exactly do I need to do about this?

4. If I'm being honest, this is certainly impacting my life.

5. Exactly how did I end up here?

After thinking back through your history, find the date and event that triggered it all. What happened that pushed "use" into "abuse," then into "addiction?" Gain awareness about your problem. Forgive yourself. Seek out help. You are far from alone. This is happening everywhere. If there is a group of people confronting you, tell them how you want their help with this. Ask them what they are willing to do. Ask someone to drive you to a facility or a local meeting happening somewhere. Ask them to help you as you find the will to help yourself.

Enduring people's intervention of you is not going to be easy. So forget that. It's going to be difficult. But let me speak to you as someone who has stood right square in your shoes and situation. If you are not willing to get the wake-up call from them, there will be another intervention to get your attention--a divine one--but it will hurt like hell. And that's going to be a whole lot harsher than this one. It won't be nice and pleasant like this. Life will break you down degree by degree until it gets your full attention. And if you don't heed it then, I feel sorry for you. I feel sad for you. You are in for a rough ride, my friend--possibly a fatal one. *My advice?* Listen to the people that love you. Stop the pain now. Get help. Get healed. With guidance and with hope, you **CAN** put the pieces of your life back together again. We did it. We built from rock-bottom up. By grace... We're flying now. We're free. Let us show you how.

Ally:

When someone you know is slipping deeper and deeper into the abyss of un-admitted addiction, how exactly do you tell them? How do you let a person know you see something out of place--particularly in their personal life? There's no easy way to face and confront an addicted person. Eventually, it's just something that has to be done.

If you're in a situation with someone you need to help (or help them to get help), you "will" need to stage what's called an intervention. It's called that because you have to intervene in a momentum of self-destructive activity that is leading a person (and all connected to them) to a very bad place. If you've let the activity go on for a while without attempting to slow or stop it, it may be speeding at 100 MPH by the time you put an orange cone down. You're the orange cone. So brace yourself for full impact when you stand in the way of it. This is not going to be an easy thing for you, nor an easy thing for them to receive. However, if you're skillful, thoughtful, prepared and heart-filled, things will go a lot better. Trust me.

You could lose the entire battle by the way you come off during an intervention. You want to realize that this battle is not a battle with them. You want to realize this is an issue you both have to overcome together. My advice is to professionally anchor yourself with the help of a good counselor or therapist who knows this terrain. Have a trusted and impartial friend to talk to during this chapter of your life. Be very prayerful about it. And after you're anchored (having found a sturdy emotional place about it all), try approaching the close family member, friend, or peer. Approach them from that healthy place you've created in yourself.

This is beyond important. Do what you must do with an extraordinary love surging in your heart. This is going to help *you* deal with the frightening difficulty of the situation. This is going to help *them* deal with the frightening difficulty of the situation. The loving confrontation could fall apart if something in you suggests negativity or condemnation--or any other gunk from unresolved issues around the regular relationship. Be respectful of the dilemma you're in. What you do or say could push them further into the isolation and the hidden life they've kept from you. You want to HELP them with the issue instead of isolate them more. You don't want to lose them. You want to love.

Ironically, when confronting someone about their addiction you actually should not be "confrontational." Confrontation does not have to be a bad experience when you are strategic and compassionate with what you are saying. Sit down with them in love; have an actual loving conversation. DO NOT come from condemnation. The person is already in self-condemnation; that is why they are using. Pouring more condemnation upon them is like pouring jet-fuel on an already 5-alarm fire--expecting the flames to go out. Curb your hurts, emotions and disappointments. Be wiser than that. Be more loving than that.

Make sure the first three words out of your mouth are loving ones. Meaning: "I love you." Make sure the first three phrases out of your mouth are ones that lift the person up. Make sure those phrases contain adjectives about the person's best human qualities and accomplishments. As you see them soften upon hearing words that lift them, gently start to address the issue at hand--all while reminding them they are better than this activity, more valuable than this activity, and can ultimately get free of this activity. Again, let them know how much they are absolutely loved.

It is highly important to start off with a positive before you start pointing any fingers at any faults. In fact, never address the addiction as a *"personal"* fault. Address it as a disease taking advantage of them. Always edify the person, separating them from the toxic activity. Show them how *they,* and *it,* are two different things. It is like condemning the sin (the disease) and not the sinner (the afflicted). You really have to separate those two ideas and concepts. The disease is one thing. The person is another. This helps you. This helps them.

Over the years our society's attitude has conflated the idea of addiction with a person's character and worth. But we don't do that with other diseases. Do we? We should not do that here. We have to give people the safety and compassionate space to come out of the shadows and get the help they need. If they feel condemned, judged and rejected by society about the disease, they will never come out of hiding and seek the help they need. People die because of this.

Intervention is not *confrontation.* Being confrontational is the opposite of what you should be when encouraging an addict to seek help. Remembering addiction is a chronic brain disease is key. Would you be confrontational or compassionate toward a loved one with advanced stages of cancer? Trust me. Firm, but loving, is the way.

Clinician:

When those in your community know you are a professional recovery counselor, they will seek your advice about what to do when in this situation. When I'm approached by people wondering how to stage an intervention,

I try to simplify it all. I try my best to put them at ease. I try not to bog them down with too much info or advice. First, I let them know they don't have to be a trained clinician to pull this off successfully; I remind them this only seems second nature to me because it's the work I do day in and day out. I tell them if it all seems too complicated to take on, use the following rule of approach.

1. Approach your loved one or friend in the way you'd want to be approached
2. Approach them with respect.
3. Approach them with honor for their soul's worth
4. Approach with gentleness toward a beleaguered and fractured ego
5. Approach them with a compassionate generosity of spirit

I encourage them. I tell them that if they can do this **authentically**, it will be felt; it will be more powerful than anything a professional could offer at that moment. Words from loved ones land in a way that words from professionals cannot at certain times. When approached by friends, family members or even co-workers about how to intervene with addicted loved ones, remind them they are armed with the most potent healing tool of all--a deep and genuine love for that person.

To Recovery:

Remember: You're not there to take inventory of that person's character. That's God's job. You're just there to gently share with them what you see--because addiction is one of the most blinding blindspots a human being could ever deal with. These substances are built to mentally and perceptually impair a person. Don't be appalled or get mad when the addict doesn't see what you see, at first. Give them time. Allow people the loving opportunity to go back and examine themselves, their lives, and how they are conducting it. When they get to the crossroads within (realizing they need help) be ready. Start investigating reputable recovery resources now. Have them on file. Have a bag already packed and stored. And when that time comes, take them right away.

RECOVERY PEARL:

"Confront with compassion."

Chapter 9

Detox vs. Recovery: The Difference?

"Don't just treat the addiction, treat what drove the person to the addiction. And that's a chronic state of hopelessness."

- Lucy Hall

CHAPTER 9

Detox vs. Recovery: The Difference?

This is one of the most commonly misunderstood things: The difference between *Detox, Abstinence,* and *Recovery*. At our facility we repeatedly work with people in our care to sharply distinguish the difference between "sober" and "recovery." We help them understand that the successes of this process won't happen overnight. "Staying stopped" isn't an instant accomplishment. Detox is the achievement of abstinence. After achieving abstinence, we explain, *recovery* is something they'll be putting their energy into for a long time. And if they are lucky, that will be the rest of their lives.

Illustration:

At my bottom, the parole officer offered me a rehab program versus jail. I took it. I knew nothing about rehab, recovery, detox, nor the difference. Substance abuse was just the way life was done as far as I was concerned. I was so green, I didn't know enough to lie to the parole officer when asked if I were a drug user. I really did think it was a normal thing. That's how messed-up I was. I had recently given birth. I had an infant child to care for. But my whole life was still about getting high. I was being saved by that parole officer's invitation to rehab. It was divine intervention, but I didn't know that then. I just wanted her off of my back. I was just agreeing to show up for this *rehab crap* on Monday to keep from being thrown in jail. It was Friday.

I spotted a Macy's on my way into her office. And I left straight out of that parole officer's office, went right across the road to Macy's, then started scamming them again. I still needed money. I still needed to get high. It was Friday night. I got high all weekend long. It was all a blur. Monday came.

I travelled to White Plains, New York for a detox program at a hospital. That's when my journey with substance abuse counseling really began--it began with me as an addict and someone else having compassion for how out-of-control I was. I told my very first counselor in rehab that my hugest fear in life was around my 7-month-old daughter. I fully expected to die from addiction, like my mother, and never see my child grow up. I'll never forget how that counselor responded. He turned to me and said, "Lucy, you are going to die, for sure. But you do not have to die like your mother died." It struck me to the core. That was a powerful turning point for me. They officially had my attention. How was it possible that I didn't have to die early like my mother?

After some weeks, the counselors could clearly see that I had a much deeper addiction problem than first assumed. A short detox program was certainly not going to do it. I don't know if it "does it" for anyone. They knew I needed more. I needed a thorough scrubbing, a rewiring of my entire mind. I needed *recovery*. They started making another plan for me. A more comprehensive one.

They decided to ship me off to another place--a long-term treatment place in upstate New York (the ultra cold and rural part). It was a place called St. Joseph's. It was in Saranac Lakes, New York. Ironically, I sit on the Board of Directors for St. Joseph's today. Just that fact within itself amazes me.

I was in treatment there for seven long weeks. The counselors knew my troubling case well. They also knew I needed a continuum of care. Wisely, they now decided I needed to go to a halfway-house in Schenectady, New York.

I was scared to death. I did not want to go to a halfway-house and definitely did not want to go to Schenectady. I was so afraid.

I found a chapel at St. Joseph's and began praying *so hard* you would have thought I was one of Jesus' disciples. I yearned earnestly, *"God I don't know what's about to happen to me, but I know you are real! Please show me a sign that I'm going to be okay!"* And with God as my witness, a sudden cool breeze blew across the pews in that chapel. And before you ask, no, I was not high. I was months into a clean life for the first time in my life. Meanwhile, it was now summer outside. And all I could hear in my frightened mind was, *"Don't let go of my unchanging hand."* I can remember that moment as clear as I can remember what I had for lunch today.

Once in Schenectady, I was assigned to a real, physical house--a halfway house. It was actully more than just a name. There were thirteen of us who lived there. Bedrooms had been converted to dorm rooms. There might have been four bunks to a bedroom depending upon the size of a room. It was like being in camp. While there, I participated in all of the programs they requested I join. I didn't resist anything. I just went along. By then I knew I was going to be alright. And I was. I never looked back. As I completed milestone after milestone I slowly started to learn the difference between treatment and recovery. If I had been shipped back to Tuckahoe after that first little detox program, I'm certain I would have picked right back up where I left off--living the life of a struggling addict--marching toward a certain death. My daughter would have been without a mother in more ways than one. For me, the difference between detox and recovery would have been the difference between life and death.

Addict:

So you completed a 3-day or 28-day detox program. Great. But think about it. You've been using how long? Oh really? And you thought this was over? You thought you could ride off into the sunset? Well, you can, my friend. But not quite the way you were thinking. Being enrolled in (or graduating from) a treatment program is just not enough. When I was sitting in my own rehab program, they told our entire group that ONLY ONE of us was going to be clean by the same time next year. That's a helluva statistic isn't it!? I made absolutely sure that ONE CLEAN PERSON was going to be me! And it was. You have to summon that same kind of resolve in the recovery process of your own life. This is far from over after detox.

If you've recently achieved sobriety in detox program and have enrolled in a treatment program, I applaud your recent accomplishments. But listen to me. Keep going! Don't stop! It is an impressive victory. I know what you had to go through just to get *there*. But you now have a brand new victory to attain. You have a new goal--a fresh new recovery process ahead of you. And it's not the kind of program you begin and end. It has no completion date. It's a one-day-at-a-time, lifelong, lifestyle--we call it "longterm recovery." Treatment is over. It's time for the next level. RECOVERY.

After a rehabilitation program of any length, when you return to real life there will be no more counselors hovering over you checking your day-to-day progress. The training-wheels will be off. You'll be back in the jungle of things--amidst predators like "temptation" and life's parade of "emotional triggers." They devour too many to count. And if you want to stay clear of their fangs, you must take on a complete and comprehensive responsibility--personally "owning" your longterm recovery process.

You now know how cunning and crafty this deathly disease can be. You should now know you will need a strategy more cunning and more crafty to keep it at bay. You must now employ a system of smart techniques to keep your recovery successes alive and gaining momentum. In short, you must now play chess with a disease. You can't play that game with just a simple and basic detox. In recovery, we will give you the rooks, knights, bishops and strategies to win your daily game against this disease. But ultimately, you must be passionately awake, alert and vigilant enough to play the game of winning your life back for good.

Ally:

Knowing this critical difference is key for every ally of the addicted. If the addict is your child, parent, sibling, friend, spouse, or co-worker, emptying that person of the drug or drink is only the first step of this work. It is not the complete work. Don't make detox your goal. Make recovery your goal for your loved one. And don't stop until you get them into a full service recovery program.

For most addicts, getting sober is not the issue. Staying clean for a while is really not that big of a deal. It's a relatively easy goal for them. It's doable. Fact is, addicts are sober all the time. It's when they get the itch to get high again--that's the problem. The true issue is learning how to identify and manage feelings, emotions and behaviors. And our work is to address and attack the "why" of that. So, at Mary Hall Freedom House, we never say that simply getting a person sober is our goal. That would be like pulling up a weed in a garden without pulling up the root--without doing the deep digging and investigations into why this weed keeps popping up over and over.

Sobriety simply defines a person's current biochemical state. Addiction, on the other hand, is about a person's compulsive thirst to misuse a substance (or activity) to their detriment. We have to truly understand the issue we are trying to tackle. And a lot of people just don't. I tell people all of the time, if they've been at my center for one day, or one-hundred days, they're already sober. The question now is: how do we finally get them transitioned into the process of recovery? How do we get them into a lifestyle of continued well-being? I have to keep reminding them that THERE IS A HUGE DIFFERENCE.

Sobriety is one plateau of accomplishment. Recovery is another plateau--a continuing one. They are two entirely different goals to meet. The second is a lifestyle change. It's shifting one's lens on life altogether. I'm constantly dismantling the misunderstanding and myth with everyone I come in contact with. Stopping the using or abusing is not the true goal. That's only temporary. **Staying stopped is the goal.** Our program's core mission is to help a recovering person build a life that is livable again--one they are not seeking a doorway to escape. Make that the goal for your loved one. (Allies: I advise you to read my coming note to fellow clinicians. There is a message for you there too.)

Clinician:

I don't think clinicians should ever boast they've gotten a person to 28 days of sobriety. Yet, many do. Getting an addict sober is only the process of teeing them up for a recovery conversation, the real shot at inner redemption and disruption of their disease. Interrupting a person's suicide for *a day* may make you a hero on the evening news, but what is going to keep that same person from getting back on the ledge the next day--after the hero and news cameras go home? That is where we should come in as clinicians. At our facility we want to restore a life from the inside-out. We want to completely destroy a person's inclination to use.

Sobering people up for a few weeks is easy cash for a lot of facilities who are singularly cash motivated. Some see the field of addiction recovery as a financially lucrative opportunity. They do not see this as the divine opportunity to save lives that it truly is. Beware of working for facilities operating from this motivation. Their choices will solely orbit around what yields them a quick financial profit versus what yields people permanent health and permanent freedom. And as a person in longterm recovery who was facing her certain death, facilities like that are a complete abomination to me. I know the difference ethical care can make. I know the devastation unethical care can leave in its wake, in a family, in a morgue. Lives can and will be lost as a result of the unwillingness to ethically give what a drowning life needs to breathe again--PERMANENTLY.

Facilities who want to make money instead of truly help people think they can substitute truth with untruths. They want to massage the egos of people in recovery to make them feel more "comfortable." They tell people what they *want* to hear instead of telling people what they *need* to hear--to be free. I always advise families, addicts and clinicians to steer clear of facilities like this. At the end of the day, these facilities will have a lot of blood on their hands. That is not a dramatization. That is a fact. Often those kinds of program structures are built to get a person off of one addiction and allow you to crutch your disease upon another addiction.

For the solely entrepreneurially inclined, I think our financial successes at Mary Hall prove there are benefits of being a God inspired and God led, ethical facility. I don't have to be conniving or clever at business. My only job is to make sure that we do the right thing: love and serve the people who walk through the doors of Mary Hall Freedom House and Freedom Village. There is a return on this kind of investment. There is a profit to this kind of program. God communicated to me "clearly" what to do, and I just want to do it. *Heal the sick. Shelter the homeless.* HE and HIS WORKS are the only business strategies I want. I can think of nothing more clever than following God's lead. And if you do not believe in God, that simply means following what is HUMANE and ETHICAL.

Please. I beg you. Don't be a sham recovery center. Had I landed on the steps of one of these facilities during my years of need, I would not have become the woman I am today. I may even be dead. And for facility owners who can see their programs reflected in the previous words, I plead with you to take a second look. I plead with you to inquire. I plead with you seek and find ways to bring more honor for human life into your programs. It is possible. You can really profit as a business and yield profit for your soul and the souls of others. I will show any clinician or facility owner how. You can get rich inside as well as out. You don't have to risk lives.

Here in Atlanta, there were a couple of pop-up flop houses (faux addiction recovery centers) so bad, that people overdosed and died right "inside" of the facility. That is how bad it can get! Mix the carelessness of a careless facility with the carelessness of an addict and ultimately people are going to die. Death by malpractice. I pray that never happens in any of our facilities. We don't allow madness inside of our programs. We do not allow the type of lackadaisical attitude in our programs that generates blatant use in our facility. We make our policies and repercussions clear. We make our dedication to client's lives CLEAR. We make the real hope for a renewed life CLEAR. I constantly pray over the ladies in our care. And I pray we stay focused and vigilant no matter how large we get. Amen.

For all facility owners and clinicians who want to do this work better, I'm a phone call away, an email away, a plane ride away.

To Recovery:

What is sobriety? "Sobriety" is only refraining from the use of psychoactive drugs or beverages. *What is recovery?* "Recovery" is when a person has entered a process to change their root thinking, not just outward behavior. It is crucially important to realize the difference between the two.

RECOVERY PEARL:

"Sobriety is a 30-day accomplishment. Recovery is a permanent lifestyle achievement."

Chapter 10

Help! They Took My Kids!

"I'm giving you hope that you can get your children back."
- Lucy Hall

CHAPTER 10

Help! They Took My Kids!

Kids are being ripped from their parents. Kids are being split up from their siblings. During this opioid epidemic there are not enough (quality) foster homes to accommodate the number of children being taken. In some areas drug abuse fuels nearly 40% of DFACS cases--where children are removed from their home. When a child is snatched from the only family it knows, the traumatic repercussions can be profound. We often have no idea how deep the scarring goes when children of addicts are forced to deal with the consequences of their parents disease. Not only are they losing the "quality" of their parent--whose cognition is impaired and dependent--but the presence of the only parent they've known. That fact can lead to those traumatized children being taken by complete strangers called "social workers," then thrust into the foster care system--a system which can often cause deeper traumas than dealing with their addicted parent. This is a problem. Solutions are needed.

Illustration:

Janice was a young woman who came to us pregnant. And I love the fact that she did. She also came to us with mental health challenges, as well as a developmental disability. Imagine those kinds of barriers set before you. Now imagine them mixed with the disease of addiction. Janice was contending with alcoholism and crack-cocaine dependency.

As you could imagine, DFACS (The Department of Family & Child Services) was ready to snatch her unborn child the moment she delivered it. They had already determined that her child would be taken and put into the foster care system. To them, she was beyond help or reach. They considered her the very definition of a "lost cause" and her case was deemed HOPE-less with a capital *"H."* But I'm not a believer in hopelessness. I'm a believer in a God who restores hope and restores life. I'm the fruit of that belief so how could I ever see anyone or any case as hopeless? I can't. I believe in miracles, primarily, because I am one. I believe in miracles because I'm LIVING one. No one could have predicted my life. I certainly couldn't have. But once my first recovery counselor planted "the hope" in me that I did not have to die like my mother did, a new me started to grow. People think Mary Hall Freedom House is just a treatment center for recovery. In truth we are so much more. We are a HOPE recovery center. We are "hope dealers." Inside the doors of Mary Hall we aim to recover every aspect of a shattered life. The number one thing we do at Mary Hall Freedom House is to bring hope to situations where there is none. It is literally our specialty.

I had to take Janice and her case by the hand. It was our job to see a possibility that no one else could--and believe in it. I remember going to Fulton County Family Court with Janice. They already knew us there and they knew our works. I made a personal appeal to them to give this young woman a chance. I wanted them to let Janice keep her soon-to-be-born child. With Janice's array of challenges, it was a hard plea to make--and surely for them, a hard plea to hear. I basically told them, "As long as Janice is in Mary Hall Freedom House and is doing well, let her keep her son, please. The last thing this woman needs is another blow of devastation, having her child taken away."

Further, we asked the courts for the detailed criteria by which Janice could possibly keep her soon-to-be-born child. Basically: We wanted to know exactly what she would have to do for the courts to consider her a fit mother?

After all of that was clear and plainly laid out, we took each point and created a comprehensive strategy for Janice. It became a main component of her personal recovery program. We worked with Janice. We supported her. And most importantly, Janice faithfully did the work of the program. She excelled and excelled. And now I am happy to report that today, Jonathan is 8-years-old. He and his mother live in our permanent housing program. They are a happy and healthy family--and they are together. Did you hear that? Janice and little Jonathan are *"together."* This is what the process of recovery makes possible. A young woman who was pregnant, developmentally challenged, had an array of mental health issues, and was alcohol and crack-cocaine dependent has recovered her life by the grace of God. Today, an 8-year old child has a mother--and a GOOD one.

Addict:

When I went to treatment for the first time, my daughter, Mary, was 7-months old. I had a lot of inner work to do. At the time, I didn't even believe I'd live long enough to watch her grow up. But my recovery counselors and coach had a different vision for me than the one I had for myself. So did God.

I had to go inside and do the work. That took courage. I had dark places and fears inside of me that had not been exposed yet. I had doors I was afraid to open. But I was the one locked on the other side of those doors. I had to work to learn how to put my fear down, put my self-loathing down, put my anger down, put my pain down. Once I put those down it was easier for me to keep putting the drugs and alcohol down. There was a better life I could live if I could turn my face to hope, to faith, to God--a Higher Power than myself. And it just worked.

Remember, I told my very first counselor in rehab that my biggest fear in life was that I was going to die from addiction, like my mother--and not see my daughter grow up. He turned to me and said, *"Lucy, you are going to die, for sure. But you do not have to die like your mother died."* I had no idea how right those words were going to be.

Right now, some of you are afraid to submit to a recovery program for fear of losing custody of your kids. You're afraid the state or even a divorced spouse may take your kids. I can't lie. Those are valid fears. You could temporarily lose custody during rehab or recovery--or in the worse cases--the state will completely take kids away from a home or parent they consider a threat to the welfare of the child/children. It does happen. But know this: the state does not want to destroy families. They will be flexible with parents who are truly demonstrating a willingness to transform and recover their lives. And you do this through the process of recovery.

You are not alone. Many of us in the process of recovery were also legally forbidden to see and/or care for our own children. Let's just face the facts. We are no good as parents when we are sick with this disease. The disease of addiction touches everyone an addict is connected to; it can extremely degrade the quality of life for a child. Some of you were also the children of addicts. You know the hell it was.

When there is substance abuse in a home it elevates the possibility of child abuse, neglect, and accidental death. It elevates the possibility of domestic violence. It elevates the possibility of a lot of horrible things. A person in active addiction can have blackout episodes where anything is possible. The life of the addicted is often coupled with stints in jails or prisons. It also can result in premature death of the addict, leaving children displaced and lost in the system. These are the reasons DFACS (or DCFS) considers an addict's lifestyle as "child endangerment." And can we blame them? The disease is no joke. I know the truth of this because substance abuse left me without a mother. That pain snowballed into my own use and downfall with addiction.

Again, the state actually wants to protect your children and actually wants to keep families together. Enrolling in a reputable recovery program NOW is the best thing you can do to save your family, save your children, and permanently correct the situation. It's time to overcome the fear and just do what you have to do for the longterm welfare of your children. You really do have to look at the BIG PICTURE as much as you can. Remember: This is a disease. What would you do to secure your children's lives, futures, and welfare if you suddenly came down with a debilitating cancer, forcing you into months of chemotherapy or other treatments. In that state, you could not "properly" take care of them. What arrangements would you make for them? How would you make sure they were cared for? This is how you have to think, because addiction is a disease that debilitates your ability to administrate your mind, actions, and choices.

Single addicted parents, be proactive; make a list of all the responsible family members and friends who could responsibly care for your children while you get help. Make arrangements, if you can. Do so before a situation happens where you're found endangering the child and a neighbor calls DFACS, making the state step in. If you love your child/children, do what it takes to get it all right again. Enter recovery.

If DFACS (Department of Family and Child Services--or your state's equivalent) has already taken your children, you're going to need a lot of help to get them back--professional help. Don't panic. Don't lose hope. That is important. Don't sink even deeper into abusing from depression and guilt. That's just going to compound the problem and prolong (or prevent) the possibility of you getting your children back.

Our facility specializes in family reunification. In a lot of cases, there is a pathway to getting your children back if you are willing to do what is necessary. And sometimes "fighting for your family" is the very fire you need to enter the recovery process and permanently live the life of recovery. Many have been there. Many have gotten their children back. You can do this. Stay hopeful. Stay prayerful. Stay in recovery. Stay stopped.

Ally:

Close and extended family members can make all the difference when it comes to keeping the children of addicts out of the foster care system. Children get caught in the storm when their parent's disease turns their lives into a living hell. This kind of traumatization makes them future candidates for addiction as well. And even though the addict in your life may have also sent you through a personal hell, remember that those children are innocent and need a safe and stable place to grow amidst their own. Let's break that cycle. I am so thankful to my dad. He became the perfect example of this kind of an ally. It was truly him and my Aunt Gertrude who were the main saviors of myself and my siblings.

I was raised by a hard-working single father. He was a widower. He was forced to raise my siblings and I after addiction took my mother. They were not living together at the time of her death. Her incessant drinking and carrying-on drove him to leaving the home when I was a young girl. He had lost hope for her and he believed her family was enabling her addiction. But when she succumbed to the alcohol, he immediately came back to take care of his children. He refused to allow any of the vying family members to get us and raise us. He did it.

My father had help. It was one of my surviving aunts who gave me the partial sense of having a mother. Though her nurturance and love was only available to me when I would occasionally visit her home, it definitely had an impact in the shaping of me. I needed a mother figure. And my Aunt Gertrude was really all the mother I had left. She was a God-fearing woman who did not abuse drugs nor drink alcohol. She was a weird anomaly where I came from. She was sober. She was a single parent raising five daughters all on her own. She ran a tight ship and kept everything afloat with a sort of grace I had never seen. She would allow me to visit for sleepovers on some weekends. And that was literally everything to me.

She made me feel so included in her family. I felt like I was one of her girls. Her home, her love, the combination became like an oasis for me. She'd feed me, comb my hair, moisturize my skin. She would do all the things that only a woman could really do right. God bless my father for all he did for my siblings and I, but, in the end, he was still a man. He did not have a woman's touch. That's like a whole different universe of love compared to a man's love and caring. Her lifestyle planted a seed in my subconscious mind. It let me know that there indeed was another way--another way of living. And most importantly, every Sunday, she would take me to church for worship service. I think that *one* single act of generosity to her motherless niece, dropped the profound anchor in my life that is still holding me down to this day--and always will. She introduced me to God. And what an introduction it was. Later in life, that seed of faith blossomed in my life in a way that keeps on giving and giving. But, Lord knows the devil was going to have his way with me first. And it doesn't matter. God won.

I shared my personal story for all of you possible allies. Some of you are family members of addicted persons. Some of you are friends. I just wanted you to see, in me, how much of a difference you could make for children whose parents are swept away by this disease. I was too young to truly understand what I was experiencing at the time. But looking back, I now see the influence it had on me. I'm now clear that my saving grace throughout my formative years was my father's hard work and commitment to keep all of my siblings together as one family--plus those powerfully loving weekends with my Aunt Gertrude. This is the kind of hope and contribution you can bring to situations that seem hopeless.

Clinician:

At Mary Hall, we understand that a lot of lives are riding on the quality of care and instruction we give. It's not just the recovering person in our care, it's the whole tribe of people they are connected to. We are dedicated to treating the whole person and the whole life that comes with them. Addiction has a familial pattern when left to its own devices. When treating an abusing parent, we know it's our opportunity to break a cycle of addiction or prevent one. We do all we can to reunify families in a healthy way. That's why our vision is to create a "village" where recovering moms and children can live together in a safe, healthy, recovery focused environment of individuals who are seriously healing and putting their lives on track. As caregivers we must help recovering persons complete treatment powerfully and meet all the measures for possible family reunification. Simply said: help them rebuild, cultivate and demonstrate sound parenting skills again so they can get their children back. Families should be "together."

To Recovery:

You may think that your addiction is only affecting you. It's not. Addiction is contagious. It has a vicious cycle. It has a way of being passed to children. It passes genetically. It passes through observation and imitation and subconscious parental role-modeling to the child. It also passes by the child's experienced trauma due to a parent's addiction, causing the child to seek psychoactive substances to escape their painful emotions. The best thing you can do to help your child is to PUT YOURSELF IN RECOVERY. It will stabilize your child's current life and lessen the chances that child will repeat or imitate your errors in judgment while dealing with this disease. Find a center. Get help now.

RECOVERY PEARL:

"Save your children. Recover."

Chapter 11

What to Do After Detox?

"It's never about the addiction.
It's about the wound triggering the addiction."
- Lucy Hall

CHAPTER 11

What to Do After Detox?

The short answer: Keep it moving. Forward, forward, forward! Get connected to a 12-Step meeting. Run as fast as you can to the nearest longterm recovery program and enroll. The point is to "keep moving progressively forward." Completion of a detox program is not a recovered life. Far from it. Detox only readies you to tackle the real work of fully recovering your life. Mistakenly thinking you're healed after a few days or weeks of sobering up can be a fatal mistake. It makes you a prime candidate for relapse. *What to do after detox?* Take on *recovery* before addiction returns with more ferocity.

Illustration:

One day I was talking with a faith partner from a local women's ministry. She came to see me with what appeared to be a pressing matter. She looked to be brainstorming how I could expand the housing component of the Mary Hall Freedom Village. She wanted to know how our program could offer more units of sober living to more affected people--specifically--units for people coming out of other treatment programs. She was asking if there was any way we could be more supportive to the overall community, by expanding our recovery "village" housing program to their affected members--plus others. I'm a pretty open minded person, so I took the time to give her a fair listen.

To further make her case, she shared a very troubling story. It was about a woman who attended their bible study the prior week. She said the woman from bible study emotionally confessed the distressing predicament she was facing. And upon hearing the woman's heartfelt plea, my faith partner was clearly deeply affected. At the end of their bible study the distressed woman erupted in tears. She told the group she was at the end her time at a local rehab facility, and had no place else to go. In other words, she was about to be homeless. This was completely heartbreaking to the churchgoers at the bible study--and it should have been.

I decided to be candid with my visiting faith partner. I let her know, as a professional, I squarely lay the blame for that predicament upon the clinicians, directors and designers of that particular rehab program. Hearing about that woman's horrifying circumstance deeply pained me. When I see a person trying to pull themselves up in the recovery process, I'm always clear that I'm looking at my own reflection. That woman is me at a different time in my life, desperately trying to cross the same bridge that got me to where I am now.

Seeing how this woman was handled made me want to double-down on how we do things at Mary Hall Freedom House. We make sure things like that do not happen. When the proper work is done up-front in the recovery process, those kinds of events should never occur. At the very beginning of a program there should always be an inquiry--an entry interview. It should be discovered whether the person is without a home, or living with an abuser, and what their post-program living options actually are. Every program should want to know if the person in rehab might be entering situations that could completely unravel their new found progress. And if that is the case, alternative options must be worked out before that person exits the program. This is just the humane way of doing things. I consider it extremely unethical to allow a person in any kind of rehab to get within two weeks of graduation and there not be a clear, solid, workable exit-plan for where that person goes afterwards. It's the rehab program's job to help the recovering addict develop that solid plan--a plan figuring out how to get back into the real world in a way that continues their newfound success. There must be an "aftercare plan" or "discharge plan" or that person will be right back where they started--distressed and picking up because of it. The situation was heartbreaking and should never happen at all. I just see that as a blatant act of malpractice.

Addict:

What is your after-treatment plan? Did you and your counselor develop a discharge/aftercare plan as a roadmap to your continued success? Did they give you a workable strategy for how to live the next phase of your life free of illicit substance use? If not, there is a problem.

Listen. If you just finished a detox program, *congratulations; I applaud your accomplishment. I*t just cleaned and prepared you for the journey of recovery. It's time to take the next step. Recovery is where true freedom from this disease lives.

As a recovery program owner, I am dedicated to helping every person in our recovery program figure out how to walk away from any service we provide never needing a Mary Hall Freedom House again. This is about recovered life! You can't just walk into our doors and say to me that you've just shown up for addiction treatment--or that you've just shown up because you have been using heroin, or smoking crack cocaine, or abusing alcohol--or even that you've shown up because the courts said you cannot have your kids back until you prove you've gotten clean and sober. As a recovery professional, I'm not going to let you get away with that level of simplification of your problem.

In our recovery program, we are not just trying to run dope and alcohol out of your veins, we are set up to run pain and hopelessness out of your life. When you show up at the doors of the Mary Hall Freedom House, we want to know if you are homeless. We want to know if you have a job. We want to know when, where, how the physical, mental or emotional abuse started. We want to know you from the inside-out because we're trying to get to the root cause of your addiction--not just clean up your external addicted behavior. That's a promise. If you've recently completed a detox, drop everything and find recovery individuals that reflect the principles and values described. Connect your life with others who have lived experience--your recovering peers. Put your life in the right hands.

Ally:

For those of you who do not understand why the dilemma of the woman from the Illustration is such a big deal, let me explain. This is important for women, men, children, everyone. Failure to have this woman's housing situation decided, after her exit from the program, is a colossal blunder. This is because the condition of homelessness is a humongous threat to her post-graduation sobriety. That kind of stress could be an enormous trigger for a recovering addict. It is not acceptable--especially when there is a claim of real care and concern for the life and well-being of the individual. We can't always provide the direct solutions to a person's life dilemmas, but we should always have a network of sources, or specialists that we can direct them toward to get to that solution. It's these kinds of facilities and situations that inspired me to create Mary Hall Freedom House with the systems it has.

In our programs we spend a great amount of time finding these kinds of resources for our recovery clients. This is compassion, but a highly professional compassion. Again, we recognize that helping recovering people stabilize their daily lives and obliterate the emotional triggers that cause them to choose to use, is a huge part of achieving a long-term addiction free life.

Beware of the treatment programs that focus on the wrong things. Too many only fixate on the substances addicts get addicted to. We focus on the traumatized soul who gets addicted to them. If you do not treat the damaged, *addicted brain*, you will soon swap out one addiction scenario for another, because the compulsive abuse of things becomes the way you do life. Finding lesser addictions that are operating in your life is also key.

TREATMENT IS A BEGINNING, NOT AN END. THIS WORK IS A BIGGER PROCESS THAN MOST THINK. I remind you; after I shed my addictions to cocaine and alcohol, I had to continue the recovery journey by shedding my addictions to things like cigarettes and even food. You must understand that the substance abuse is only a symptom to the neurological disease that addiction is. You must SOLVE THE ADDICTION MENTALITY not just the activity. The dysfunctional activity is only a symptom of neurology. Cocaine use was not my disease. Alcohol use was not my disease. THE NEUROBIOLOGICAL ASPECTS OF THE ADDICTION BRAIN was (and still could be) my disease. I misused substances and activities to medicate my emotions in a compulsive neurological disorder. I became obese, compulsively gorging on food, until a hundred pounds over-weight, until I shed that addiction too. I had to learn how not to mismanage my emotions and how not to use outside substances as a crutch to avoid feelings. This work is not a "detox." Detox leads to "re-tox" without managing the disease of addiction. "Retoxification" is eminent if you do not address what is driving the compulsion to abuse things and self. *What to do after detox or treatment?* All of the aforementioned is what I did. Recovery is what I live. Recovery is what I do. Anyone who says detox or treatment is enough, don't fall for it. Don't let your loved ones fall for it.

Clinician:

For many clinicians and facility owners, all of this just seems like a lot of extra work--and it is. But it does not occur to us as extra work because it is a part of our stated credo, our vision, our purpose. Many years ago I had to decide what we were going to be about at Mary Hall Freedom House. And what I've described above was absolutely it. I wanted to duplicate my personal success as a recovered person in others--over and over and over. Having lived this, I knew (and know) what's possible. The choices were and are clear; we could half-ass this and screw over a lot of lives, or we could be about something more compassionate. I chose the latter. I had to figure out how we do this mission, internally, and who we needed to partner with externally to get it all done. So we consider it our daily work to at least "attempt" to address the complexity of the lives of the people we serve--in order to give them the greatest chance at achieving a restored life. And hey... We don't always win, but a lot of times we do. We're not geniuses over here, we just care. WE ARE HOPE DEALERS WHO CARE! This is what I want to inspire in our industry as a whole.

To Recovery:

The more the years go on, it seems all of the specialists, scholars and researchers are catching up with the things I've been saying all along. I guess when you're a former addict from a family of addicts, you can't really get more specialized than that. Right?

Today, a lot of leading thinkers on this subject have found that addicts' abuse of a controlled substance is not truly for love of the substance at all--which I've been confessing and preaching forever. The substance is just a doorway for an addict to temporarily escape a burning building--and that building is their lives. The problem is, of course, that door is a temporary exit--a highly destructive exit, adding flames to a life that is already burning down.

There's nearly a consensus about the emotional states that lead us to seek, obtain and ingest psychoactive substances we know are harmful to our personal health, families and overall lives. Speaking as a recovered person, I am a part of that professional consensus--and I admit that a professional must thoroughly understand these emotional states in order to help someone pull themselves out of the depths of addiction. Never think a 5 to 28–day detox program is enough. It is not. There must be a detox from the states of being which made the addiction possible in the first place. Find a recovery center that treats the whole issue--one that treats your whole LIFE itself.

RECOVERY PEARL:

"It's never about the drug. It's about the pain
we're trying to kill WITH the drug."

Chapter 12

How to Avoid a Relapse?

"Relapse: The ever lurking enemy looking to take your recovered life away."

- Lucy Hall

CHAPTER 12

How to Avoid a Relapse?

You don't get to keep parts of the old life and also gain the new. That's not how this works. You must give your recovery respect. You must have a reverence for your recovery, a healthy respect for your disease, and deep gratitude for the grace shown to you--allowing you to escape the grips of the disease, daily. You must, must, must give your recovery that much respect.

Having this attitude is fundamental: *"I understand that my addiction is greater than me. That's how I got here. That's how I fell to such a deathly, dilapidated condition before recovery. It was greater than me. And now I've found something greater than my disease and me--the God of my understanding. I maintain a healthy fear for what brought me to my knees. I maintain a profound and ecstatic reverence for what lifted me up."*

Listen to me. Without daily reverence, relapse is inevitable.

Illustration:

I have a cousin. A cousin I've been close to all of my life. We grew up together. Around the same age. Same family lineage. Same genetics. Her drug of choice was heroin. My drug of choice was cocaine. I always had to do uppers. She liked downers. I'm a *"get up and keep it moving!"* kind of personality. She's a *"sit down and let's wait" type of personality. Drug choice usually follows personality types.* I've been clean for 30 years and she'd been clean for nearly 20. She just recently returned to using. *Did you hear what I just said?*

The news of her relapse broke my heart. I was so hurt--and hurt for both of us. Listen to what I just said! 20 years! How sad! Right? This is what I mean! We can be clean for decades and mistake this issue for a "WILLPOWER" thing, and think we have two decades of demonstrated "WILLPOWER" to show that we now have the strength to manage casual use. *NO!* This was never a willpower issue--it is a disease! And that disease we left "dormant" decades ago, hasn't gone anywhere. We only worked to build a lifestyle that has left it deactivated.

Like a diabetic can adopt a lifestyle that leaves their predisposition minimized, addicts do the same. But if you abandon your "management lifestyle" for whichever disease, you have let the tiger out of the cage. Because you misunderstood the tiger. You thought it was tamed. How you live can keep it tranquilized, or stir it to ferocious activity. Never tamed.

Many misunderstand addiction. My cousin did. 20 years put her into a false sense of complacency. Think of the many who take tigers or lions as pets, and think the tigers have forgotten they are tigers just because the human has forgotten. They get complacent. They stop taking precautions around a dangerous animal. They get comfortable. They presume the animal is their friend. And on one unpredictable day that presumption gets them mauled. Unfortunately, this is what I'm watching happening to my relative. It's like a powerful warning shot to all in her recovery community. It's a reminder to us all that this "insidious disease" is not to be played with. My cousin is being taken down by addiction again--right in front of me. The threat of relapse is real--because this disease is real.

Addict:

My cousin is not an anomaly, but it still hurts. SO MANY PEOPLE GET EMOTIONALLY TRIGGERED BY LIFE AGAIN. Somewhere along their path, life happens--and if they don't have a contingency plan to deal with difficult emotions--they start picking up again. Life is not going to stop happening just because you're in a recovered life. You got to be wise! You got to go DEEP into your recovery practice and forever be ready. I keep telling people over and over that we must arrive in the abstinence category for the right reasons. We cannot just do the "abstinence" thing and not do the "recovery" thing. If we stop the dope and never clean out the closet of all the issues that drove us to use the dope--guess what--it's coming back. You must, must, must deal with 'why' that first hit felt so good to you when you took it. You must deal with all of your traumas, your pains, your insecurities, your inadequacies and your mental imbalances. This is the difference between getting stopped for a period of time, versus, adopting the recovery lifestyle. Deal with the triggers, beloved. Not just the use. Heal yourself for real.

I've been at this for three decades and I still do not cut myself any slack. Slack is the precursor to doom. I don't allow it. I love my life and I don't want to do one single solitary damned thing to jeopardize it. I monitor myself like crazy. I monitor my emotions like crazy. *I stay awake--awake about my disease.* Because "emotions" are the place where it all starts. So I stay vigilant with a capital "V." Respect this disease.

Ally:

I want to give you an expanded understanding so you can have an expanded love for the recovering person in your life. This is important because you will be key to helping them remain vigilant about their disease for the rest of their lives--no matter how long it's been since they've picked up. The traps of a lackadaisical attitude must be avoided. This goes for all--allies plus persons in addiction recovery. One of the hugest traps that people (addicts, family members and friends) fall into is failing to embrace the fact that this is a disease. No matter how many years it's been, never question why they still need to attend 12-step meetings or why they can't have just one drink. *Why?* Because "one is never enough," and "meeting makers make it." Period.

The addict at most risk will say to you, "Oh, it's just willpower. I got this now." Listen: *No, it's not, and no they don't.* Never believe that addiction is about willpower. It is not. It is about a brain that is excessively wired for compulsive behavior--not willpower. Never let your guard down. If you've ever seen the things that a strung-out person in active addiction will do to get what they need to get that high, you would know that WILLPOWER is the last thing an addict lacks. Addicts get their fixes by any means necessary--with every ounce of will, skill and wit at their disposal. So, what's really lacking? For the addicted, what's lacking is the FULL acknowledgment and personal understanding that they indeed carry a physiological disease. Therefore there is a failure to treat what they're carrying like one--failing to seek and employ the measures to manage it.

The reason people think this issue is psychological is because the physiological takes over the psychological in those in whom this disease is activated. I see where they make their mistake. But that small misunderstanding can be a fatal mistake for some. Let's tell the truth. Non-addicted people are often really secretly thinking that addicts are CHOOSING to be addicts. But, wait. Think with your better mind. WHO CHOOSES to be an addict? Who in the hell would WANT that life? The first hit may be a choice. But the choices after that, for many, are already chosen. It's like all of a sudden you find out that you have something in your body, creating a chemical phantom--a phantom that you find yourself chasing over and over and over again. It is the scariest thing.

Clinician:

WE MUST TEACH THE REAL! Even though we give lots of hope at our facility, we do not sugar-coat the reality of what our clients are facing. People need to hear the REAL about the disease they are battling. This is the only way they can properly prepare for that fight. In my first program as an addict, the truth of that reality never became clearer than that day I was sitting in my own rehab program (scratching my way to freedom) and that counselor audaciously said, "I can tell you right now, that out of all of you in this room, ONLY ONE of you is still going to be clean by next year this time." As I mentioned earlier, that put the FIRE OF DETERMINATION in me to be THAT ONE. When I heard those painful words something leapt into my soul. I wanted to tell everyone in that room that ONE CLEAN PERSON was going to be me. And it was. It absolutely was--by God's grace. And let me tell you... RAW TRUTH can help a recovering person summon that same kind of resolve in their own life's recovery. Give them the unadulterated truth so they can be THE ONE too. Be real about this disease with the people you are treating. It may be the very thing that saves them.

To Recovery:

This disease deserves your constant vigilance, your constant respect. Underestimating it can be deadly. Five or even fifty-years sober is no cause to get relaxed about your disease. Should a surviving cancer patient suddenly stop the healthy lifestyle activities helping keep them alive and cancer free? Addiction is complex, baffling and extraordinarily cunning. It hurt me so deeply to see my cousin succumb to drug abuse again after decades of being free. I cannot describe the pain of that. But it was also a divine reminder to me, about the grace I've been shown--plus the sheer gamesmanship of this puzzling disease. It reminded me that even after 30 years clean, I must remain as vigilant as I was when I was only 30 days clean. This is how to live a life in recovery. And for me, God, is my whole armor, everyday. I pray to remain His miracle--for me, and for others.

RECOVERY PEARL:

"Know thy enemy. Respect thy enemy. Addiction is thy enemy."

Chapter 13

Helping Loved Ones in Recovery

"Help, but never turn one victim into two."
- Lucy Hall

CHAPTER 13

Helping Loved Ones in Recovery

Though addicted persons lead secret lives to support their secret (or not so secret) addictions, signs are always there. Alert spouses, family members, or friends notice. Abrupt changes in behavior or personality patterns are always first indicators. When loved ones become withdrawn, erratic, compulsive or suddenly secretive, pay close attention. Something is going on. If your worst suspicions are confirmed one day, and you decide to help them, brace yourself. Your life may not be the same again for quite some time. It may very well become a hurricane of drama. It's going to take a lot of love, prayer and self-care to see this through.

Illustration:

A production crew filled our recovery facility at Mary Hall Freedom House. They were shooting a documentary on the work we do. Little did we know, things were about to fall completely apart. Everything had been running so smoothly until everything just wasn't. We were on schedule. We were on track. But a huge derailment was on the way due to the disease of addiction. And I had no idea that this particular chapter subject was about to become front-and-center while I was writing this book. But that's how life is. That's how God is.

Out of the blue, I received a call from the executive producer of the film. He seemed a bit frantic, a little unhinged--which was highly unusual. This guy was always mega positive, pragmatic, about business and cool as a cucumber. I knew something was up. After a few sentences it was clear this wasn't a business call. He was seeking my professional counsel. He began explaining he'd just been thrown into the depths of some emotions he was just not used to dealing with. It was after receiving a highly distressing voicemail. It was about his father.

His father had just crashed (and totaled) the car he had recently bought for his dad. The landlord of the apartment complex where his father was living called the son. He was threatening to evict his dad, begging the producer to come get his father immediately. But the producer was on the other side of the country at this time, in Atlanta, with us. His father was in L.A.

According to the landlord's call, the father had been walking around the "child friendly" apartment complex nearly nude, parading his exposed sexual organs before residents, and entertaining prostitutes all day and night with his V.A. checks. On top of that, the father had had a string of dramatic visits from the L.A. Sheriff's department. In addition, the producer had just learned local gang members were threatening to kill his father. His father had gone from model citizen to neighborhood menace in the blink of an eye.

His father, who had been clean and free of alcohol abuse for years, and prior to that, cocaine, was suddenly using again. After two years of freedom he had a ferocious relapse. He was burning his life down again--all while his son was producing a film on addiction recovery. How's that for irony?

A lot of addicts are the equivalent of Dr. Jekyll and Mr. Hyde when using versus not using. They swing from one extreme personality to another. This was certainly the case the producer's father. Off psychoactive substances, he was a mild-mannered and beloved school teacher and retired military veteran. On psychoactive substances, he was a terror to his community, family and self. This is not unlike many people in active addiction.

Everything halted. The crew had to go home. Documentary production was put into emergency suspension for an entire quarter. Over the next months, I watched the producer pause his career and family life to enter the eye of the storm. His mission was to help his dad and clean up the devastation this latest relapse was leaving in its wake. It became a wild goose-chase--crazy drama after crazy drama--spanning over multiple cities. There were insurance claims to file, multiple police reports, multiple arrests and bail-outs from various jails in Nevada and California. It also became about removing his father from the gang's reach. There was re-location arrangements to administrate, constant calls to institution after institution, and a trail of broken relationships.

The producer had gotten his father into that apartment because of a longterm friendship with the owner of the complex. That friendship was strained and likely severed for good. He called lists of relatives in other cities for help, but no one wanted to deal with this again. He was on his own, with some help from his brother. And this went on for months. By storm's end the producer realized his family had just burned through $20K putting out the latest fires of his father's addiction.

The situation wasn't really new. The emotions were new. The film producer had been taking care of his father's issues since 16-years old. He explained he'd been more of *the father* and his father had been more of *the son* during their entire relationship. In many ways his father had always been a "dependent." But now the producer had his own family to care for--a wife, a mortgage and two wonderful sons. At what point does one stop extinguishing the fires in the never ending saga of an addicted parent's life, before one's own life begins to burn down too? Good question.

When the next call came from a random little town in central California, saying they'd taken his father into custody, he traveled there. He saw the condition his father was in. Naked, defecating in the cell, erratic and aggressive with officers, off of his mental health meds--the father was probably the lowest he had ever seen. Over the months, the father had fought and destroyed every solution the son tried to bring. There were many. It was a sad moment. The producer knew what he had to do. There was no choice. He was left with no choices because ultimately the choice to recover and save one's life has to come from the addicted person themselves. Many allies learn this over time, and it's an expensive lesson.

Eventually our documentary got back on track later in the year. Filming resumed. Our producer poured his heart out trying to help his father. He did the best he could. He stayed in contact with the authorities letting them know all of the vital medications his father needed. But it was clear he had to let go. He had to let his father go through the process of hitting rock-bottom again. And it was a very rocky bottom this time. He knew his father might not live through this one. When relapse happens, addiction always seems to come back seven times worse. Remember that.

Addict:

Deepen yourself in the practices of recovery. Build a firewall around yourself against this disease. Never go easy. Never think you've made it to the other side. There is no other side. Recovery is the life we live from now until the day we're done. You're a disease manager. I'm a disease manager. And I'm a Hope Dealer. I keep what I have by giving it away. I'm blessed to be a blessing. I'm a disciple of Christ and Recovery. We are forever co-workers at this.

I will say it again: Addiction is cunning and baffling. It is perplexing and unforgiving. It didn't matter that the producer's father had been clean for years, living independent again, holding down a prime job. Addiction doesn't care. When we allow this disease to be triggered, it takes over everything. If we start feeling better and stop taking our meds--thinking we are normal and all better and can live like other people, we have turned down the wrong road of thinking. A crash is coming. No matter how many years clean you achieve, you can never let your guard down. You must live the life. You must practice the practices. You must become the principles of recovery every single day of your life without fail--with zero vacations from it. It just has to become your way of life. There is no *I'm clean and I'm all better now, so I can relax.* No, beloved. It is not that kind of disease. You are managing an ongoing condition. You will never get 50 years clean and then be considered cured. No--it does not work that way.

A person may be successfully managing diabetes for 30 years, feeling good, feeling healthy. But they can't just all of a sudden eat a whole bag of sugar without sending themselves into an immediate diabetic coma. We must live with a lifestyle that completely respects the disease we are carrying whether it is active in us are not. Don't let the illusion of a zillion years clean make you think the disease is gone. It's not.

Ally:

The producer's father was clean and living a good life. He was actually doing great. His life had become what we might call "normal." He was happy and had settled into a productive life routine. But the addiction neurology hadn't gone anywhere. The entire new life the producer helped to build around his dad went up in flames. Whenever the good life returns there is a seductive pull to believe the disease is gone. Ally and addict alike must forever remain cognizant of this and not be swayed. Remain vigilant about your loved ones.

In the illustration, the devastating relapse left the son suspended between loyalties to his father versus loyalties to his son's futures. How many times was he to take 20k away from his sons' college futures? All the resources, all the love, and all the loyalty could not save an individual who was not ready to be loyal to self and the lifestyle of recovery again. And no matter how faithful an ally you are to an addicted person, no man knows that day. No man can force that day. The addicted person has to make a choice to recover.

It's hard to know when to get more deeply involved and when to pullback. Sometimes the help and support of dedicated loved ones is the only thing standing between an addict and the grave. But if you are that ally, you must learn to be a smart ally. Help but help with healthy boundaries. If you are dealing with an addicted loved one, I don't know where your line is but there is one. And you should know where it is. Sharply define it. When circumstances cross that line, you have to make the hard choice to preserve your own life. You just can't let yourself get pulled into the flood waters while trying to pull someone else out of them. You could capsize yourself and your whole family, drowning everyone. Remember: *"To thine own self be true."*

When you love an addicted person, it is far from easy--because it is like you are not dealing with the person you've always known and loved. If you've ever been the child of an addicted parent you already know the following truth: once a person starts abusing a substance, their psychological age gets totally arrested. They stop growing. Actually, they start to regress. *"I"* was the child of an addicted parent. I watched my mother stop growing and become the worst version of herself. *"I"* was someone's addicted child plus addicted parent. I stopped growing and became the worst version of myself--the disease had broken me down.

When an active addict is going through regression, they can cause a whole lot of chaos in their lives and the lives of people who love them. That chaos becomes emotionally draining and financially draining if you let it. Be ready to deal with items stolen, their addicted friends, arrests, bail money, lawyer's fees, property damage, community embarrassments, conflicted loyalties, 4AM emergency phone calls and sometimes violence.

Be loving to your addicted family member. Be compassionate about their plight. But never violate life's core principle: self-preservation. If you cannot get their own survival instinct to kick-in, don't lose yours. If, over time, your loved one stays stuck in denial, refusing help, and you start falling into the depths with them, step back. Seek professional help yourself to recover your own sanity, health and emotional sturdiness. Don't lose your own well-being trying to save theirs. That helps no one. Letting one victim multiply into two isn't productive. Practice extreme self-care.

And remember, YOU ARE NEVER ALONE. There are countless people in your very same predicament. Resist the urge to isolate or turn this struggle into a buried family secret. There are people who intimately know your challenges. Find peer groups in your area. Give yourself that support and community. It will be healing in ways you cannot predict. Join or attend AL-ANON meetings, organized to help family members of addicts. Join or attend ALATEEN meetings, organized to help teen loved ones of addicts. Join or attend NAR-ANON meetings, organized to help loved ones of addicts. Join or attend

ADULT CHILDREN OF ALCOHOLICS meetings, organized to help adult children of addicts.

I highly recommend you become active in either of these communities. The journey is often long, rough, bumpy and sometimes cyclical. But if you anchor yourself properly, you and your loved one can make it through this. I did.

Clinician:

When family members enter our facilities to drop off addicted loved ones seeking recovery, we must pull them aside and check on their wellbeing. We must let them know how much support and help is available for them. Let them know they are not alone. Let them know their sacrifices do not go unnoticed. Host family sessions, groups and AL-ANON meetings or equivalent group meetings supporting family members and loved ones of addicts. It's needed. Have licensed therapists on file you can recommend for an addict's ally. Strengthening a recovery client's tribe is a part of strengthening them. The healthier the environment they are released into, the healthier chance they have at staying recovered and out of relapse.

To Recovery:

I would not want my children or anyone else to lose their own lives and security just because I was losing mine. I would want help to help myself, but not to their detriment. There is no use turning one victim of this disease into multiple. Allies: Be sure you are not becoming codependent in an unhealthy relationship with the addict. Dependency is dependency, whether emotional dependency or substance dependency. The goal is "health" all the way around. And co-dependency fuels and enables your loved one's substance abuse. If you feel you might be developing co-dependent traits, groups like CODA.ORG (Co-Dependents Anonymous) are also available for support. Get recovery help for them. Get recovery help for self.

RECOVERY PEARL:

"To thine ownself be true."

Chapter 14

Fixing Relationships Addiction Destroyed

"Addiction destroys all in its path."
- Lucy Hall

CHAPTER 14

Fixing Relationships Addiction Destroyed

Addiction takes the addicted person to the depths of hell. It can drag friends, family and closest associates down in the process. Relationships get destroyed. Some are recoverable. Some are beyond repair--never to be rebuilt. In our counseling classes at Mary Hall, we get to admit and confess all of the things we did to our friends, family members and community--just to get high. We get to talk about all of the things that happened--what happened to us and happened to others while we were in the grips of addiction. This purge is powerful. For some, it is their first and only opportunity to get closure, healing, and emotional resolution.

Illustration:

In some of our sessions, recovering addicts get to participate in a role playing exercise. Clients in recovery get to have imaginary conversations with all the people they have harmed during their campaign of addiction. A volunteer in the group will pretend to be the person affected by the recovering addict, while the recovering addict has a reconciliation conversation to admit, apologize and make amends for their transgressions. In some of the heaviest instances, our counselor will play the role of the affected people in the recovering addict's life as the class watches. The process is extremely confronting. But in the end, it's healing for all.

During one of our group sessions, there was a young lady who left all of us overwhelmed with tears. It had been a day of heartbreaking stories--purging, releasing, healing. But when this particular woman came to the front of the group, it changed the entire energy of the room. No one had any idea what was coming. We could tell it was something heavy. But no one knew it would be this heavy.

The woman took her place before the group. She gathered her courage. She began to speak. Word after word, every heart in the room balled into knots. Her confession was the hardest to hear. God knows it must have been hard to tell. But she got through it. She admitted that years ago, while at her bottom (using to live and living to use), her addicted condition and carelessness led to her 15-year-old being raped and murdered by her boyfriend of the time.

Everything in the room went silent.

This woman had to carry a tremendous burden of guilt, blaming herself for her daughter's horrifying death. I couldn't imagine walking around with that kind of pain in me. My heart still sinks for her.

We had to play the role of her murdered child and have the confrontational therapy conversation with her. It was exceedingly difficult. In cases like that, we pray to say the right words that will cause healing and not further injure the burdened soul.

On the surface, it might seem this therapy is about the harmed people we bring into the group conversation. It is not. Confrontational Therapy, in the end, is for a different purpose. The woman will never truly have the opportunity to physically sit down and make amends with her deceased child. But the exercise is potent, necessary and powerful. Because the main destroyed relationship that all addicts must restore is the destroyed relationship with self. It's to repair what we are doing to self, inside, because of what we did to others in the diseased state. At the end of the confrontational therapy, we make amends, we hug and we look to close these highly emotional chapters of their lives.

Addict:

Being "high" means being in a state of impaired mind--impaired judgement. In this impaired mind, we make a mess of our lives and our human relationships. We not only hurt ourselves, but friends and family members. During recovery there will be a time to talk about reconnecting with them, requesting forgiveness, and correcting our wrongs. Once we return to our right mind, we not only need to repair ourselves, but these torn relationships.

This work is more about *willingness.* It does not always mean to rush out making amends with people. The sincere "willingness" alone is transformative. It's about having it in your heart, and getting emotionally clean (emotional recovery is a process as well). Some people just do not want to hear from us again. And in some cases, attempts to make amends with people in the real world could cause irreparable harm to others. For instance, admitting you slept with someone's spouse while under the influence--just to expunge your guilt--could turn their lives into a world of turmoil. Or, worse, it could get you killed. In that case, just have the willingness to make it right. And in the PROPER instances--where talking to people can make a positive difference--do so.

During this stage of recovery, we cannot forget our children. Often, they are the ones we have hurt the most. But sometimes, when making amends with your children, it's really not about words or confessions. It is just about becoming the mother or father, they always needed. They might not yet understand the complexities of adult life and adult challenges. Your confessions might be inappropriate. It is more about the softening of your heart and the transformation of your behavior. It's about who you are BEING. That, they can perceive.

For my children... it wasn't until they became of age that they understood what I was going through, let alone what I put my family through. We still have conversations about it 30 years later. It's important for me to listen to how they felt as children in my early days of recovery, and give respect to their feelings and how they were affected.

We all do or have done terrible things while under the influence. When we sober up, we realize the things we've done and want to get high again--to get away from the pain of what we've done, and who we've been, during another blackout or binge. We want to run from that reality--back to the alcohol, needle, pipe or pill. They become painkillers that create more pain, plus justification for their existence in your life. It's a vicious, nasty, ugly and even deadly cycle.

You must step away from the self-condemnation and realize it is the disease doing these acts to others and to you. If you could see the brain scans of what is happening in your brain when addiction strikes, you would physically see that it is not you, but the disease. In our program we teach a course called The Neurobiology of Addiction. Recovery clients get outside of their addiction to see it from the outside in. You cannot imagine how powerful and healing this is. When you literally see "your brain in active addiction," a lot of things become clear. Deep knowledge of this helps us rise above any self-condemnation, ending the emotional states which lead to more abuse. It helps us soften. It helps us surrender. And surrender is the ABSOLUTE ONE AND ONLY ROAD to freedom.

Trust me, I know.

That's why The 12-Steps say:

> 1. We admitted we were powerless over alcohol (and drugs); that our lives had become unmanageable.
>
> 2. Came to believe that a Power greater than ourselves could restore us to sanity.
>
> 3. Made a decision to turn our will and our lives over to the care of God as we understood Him.

4. Made a searching and fearless moral inventory of ourselves.

5. Admitted to God, to ourselves and to another human being the exact nature of our wrongs.

6. Were entirely ready to have God remove all these defects of character.

7. Humbly asked Him to remove our shortcomings.

8. Made a list of persons we had harmed, and became willing to make amends to them all.

9. Made direct amends to such people wherever possible, except when to do so would injure them or others.

10. Continued to take personal inventory and when we were wrong promptly admitted it.

11. Sought through prayer and meditation to improve our conscious contact with God as we understood Him, praying only for knowledge of His will for us and the power to carry that out.

12. Having had a spiritual awakening as the result of these steps, we tried to carry this message to alcoholics and to practice these principles in all our affairs.

Drop everything. Surrender everything. This has not been "you." This has been the disease acting "through you." Give it all away to A Higher Power and be healed. I know the way. I've walked it.

Ally:

Your consistent compassion as an ally is necessary and crucially important. And the only way to maintain it, is to accept this as a neurological disease and not as a character defect. Be ready to accept the appeals for forgiveness. Be ready to give audience to their efforts to make amends. Prep the family for this--even extended family and community. When the time comes, it will help the addict forgive themselves and achieve a clean emotional slate. This slate becomes the foundation from which they rebuild their inner-selves and possibly the relationships with the people most important in their lives.

In our recovery journey, this is just what we must do. Concentrate on these two steps when repairing relationships:

> 8. Made a list of persons we had harmed, and became willing to make amends to them all.
>
> 9. Made direct amends to such people wherever possible, except when to do so would injure them or others.

Some things we have done while under the influence will seem unforgivable. That is understandable. But remember, forgiveness does not exonerate responsibility. We just want the chance to "emotionally" start again.

Clinician:

I believe Confrontational Therapy (the therapy referred to earlier in this chapter) should be put into every recovery program. It is a powerful and deeply cathartic tool. After detoxing the chemicals from their systems, clients start to see life clearly again. They see what they've done. Remorse sets in. Release is needed. And once you open that tap, they want to disclose it all. They want the weight off of their chests from all of their impaired choices. Because of this, in our confessional and confrontational type of therapy sessions, we keep the therapy very disciplined and intentional. Clients will want the exercises to go on and on--because there is so much they want to purge from their souls. However, it takes a strong and experienced facilitator to properly and successfully hold the space for therapy like this.

I recently observed a young facilitator attempting to run a process group, but failing the group, by not adequately commanding the group. (For those unfamiliar with our field, a "process" group is where recovering addicts discuss their issues, versus a didactic group, where clinicians primarily teach useful facts and information.) A key indicator of an "inexperienced facilitator" is when they allow a sitting participant to take the entire session hostage and off message. It is a professional no-no. When it is allowed to happen--especially in an unhealthy way--it affects everyone in attendance.

I witnessed one of the participants being allowed to go on and on about a subject that had zero relevance to the process of recovery. The boisterous participant was never reined-in. Always make sure the venting is actually productive, cathartic, and carrying out the purpose of the group. Never allow grandstanding from a person who is an addict for attention. Don't forget we are in a medical process to remedy a progressive disease. Time and opportunity is precious. People require loving but rigid leadership. Without it, things fall apart quickly.

To Recovery:

Some will never forgive you. Accept that. But you must forgive yourself. Clean up the messes you can. Leave the messes you cannot, to God. You must go forward to save your life. Forgive yourself for who and what you became on psychoactive substances. You were ill. The disease was ravaging your brain. Surrender yourself to a Higher Power. Be redeemed. Recovery is the opportunity to declare a new self, build a new self and become a new self. Focus there. Start clean. Start over.

RECOVERY PEARL:

"Forgive me. Then allow me to forgive myself."

Chapter 15

Complete Recovery Takes How Long?

"The luckiest amongst us are in recovery forever."
- Lucy Hall

CHAPTER 15

Complete Recovery Takes How Long?

What exactly is "complete recovery?" What are we asking when we ask that question? I'm 30 years into my recovery and I do not understand the concept "complete recovery." What is that? I'm not a fan of these types of questions. For the person who asks how long complete recovery takes, I answer: *It takes as long as it takes.* And if you're lucky that will be for the rest of your life. Trust me. You don't want recovery to ever end. That would be called relapse. You want recovery to become your new life day in and day out until your days are done.

Illustration:

In my own beginning of the recovery process, I was being shipped to program after program. I never knew where I was going next. From the moment that parole officer signed me up, I would just go where I was told to go. I was surrendered. It was like there was a bigger process happening to me than I knew. I just knew I was not interested in looking back. I wanted freedom.

Place to place, program to program, city to city, all over New York State--I was soon to learn that addiction was a disease, not a way of life. I was soon to learn that the end result for my mother, brothers, aunt and grandmother did not have to happen to me. Death by drug overdose or alcohol was not written in stone. What a revelation! I did not have to surrender my life to that. I was about to learn there was a whole world of life that I didn't know existed as a possibility for me. I'm so thankful those people did not stop working on me after detox and a 28-day in-patient program. They had another program to send me to. I needed every last one of them. God just kept allowing doors to open for me.

I remember being shipped from White Plains, NY, to Saranac Lake, NY. It was in that program I started getting in touch with who I really was. I hadn't a clue who I was. I had no self-worth nor esteem. I was a people-pleaser--trying to be all things to all people. The staff at the treatment center diligently, lovingly, persistently worked with me until I started taking off the mask. Underneath, we found a frightened little girl who was afraid she was going to die the death of her mother. It was there that I found out I lived in constant 24/7 fear and anxiety--and had been living with that since six years old when my mother died. I lived as a nervous wreck all of my life and did not know it. Because, again, it was all that I ever knew.

Slowly, I was learning to take it all one day at a time. I spent weeks then months in programs. I was being cleaned out in ways I cannot describe. I was going through the "real" detox -- an emotional and psychological one – the real clean and sober program. These people were not committed to just stopping my alcohol and cocaine abuse. They were committed to eradicating every root and trigger I had for using it. By God's grace, they pulled all of my pieces out and rebuilt me. <u>They took away my reasons for dope and sold me on HOPE</u>. My esteem was being rebuilt. My identity was being rebuilt. My future was being rebuilt. I didn't know what was happening to me then, but looking back now, as a professional, this is what was happening to me. I was being renewed. This is what the process of real recovery looks like. I can remember it like yesterday.

Seven weeks went by. They said they were about to send me to a halfway house. I was then shipped from Saranac Lake to Schenectady, NY. I didn't know what to expect. I didn't know what was going on. I never did. I just kept surrendering and surrendering and surrendering to God. I was just following the path being laid out in front of me. What else was I going to do?

At the halfway-house, I lived college-dorm style with other women just like me. We slept in bunk-beds and lived like a large family. We were probably 10 to 13 women living In a literal house. It was beautiful. We were being taught how to live life on life's terms--while learning to live recovery one day at a time. We were being taught how to get a job, how to faithfully go to 12-Step meetings and talk about our new way of life, and how to faithfully come home. We were being taught how to have dinner as a family, and how to go to bed--and just how to live normal healthy routines of life. It was powerful.

Everyday, we would wake up together. We would eat breakfast. We would all go out to jobs and work. None of our meetings or meals were about sitting around in idle chatter. Everything was centered around recovery. As a recovery family we were actually sharing our experiences and hopes of the day. We were becoming new human beings. We were not waking up to use and using to live everyday. And when we made mistakes, our sponsors were there to hold our feet to the fire and help us make healthier choices based on their lived experience. We were learning key life skills, how to be productive members of society in this thing called life. It was great. It was life. It was life on life's terms. It was everything.

And don't get me wrong, I was no angel yet. My sainthood was still in progress (LOL). Even while in that halfway-house I had a moment of regression from my progress. Those addiction behavior habits are ingrained deeply. Looking back, I still can't believe it, but it's true. Even in the midst of all of that healing, I managed to find my way to a mall department store and stole something. I was boosting. *Again?* Can you believe that? Well, believe it. I did it. But I needed the experience. It taught me something profound. There was a difference now; I felt strange. I felt incredibly guilty about it. Eventually, I even felt awful. And it just got worse and worse. I had no peace whatsoever about it. I couldn't steal like I used to. *Wow.* I had to track down my sponsor and completely confess my crime.

Skillfully showing me how to live like a normal human being again, my sponsor said, "Lucy if you feel bad about it. Go to the store and take the item back." *Wait. What!?* That seemed ludicrous to me. "That's just not who you are anymore, Lucy. Go take it back.", said my sponsor. I felt so bad. I knew my sponsor was right.

I could not tell anyone in the halfway-house about my insane actions. So, I asked one girl who lived there with me to run over to the mall with me real quick. I couldn't tell her anything else.

She came with me. I walked into that store with that stolen item. I just pretended like I was going to exchange it for a new one. I took it up to the customer service counter, left the bag and hurriedly told the girl, *let's go!* She was confused, saying, *but what about your exchange?* I said, *shut up let's just go!*

Let me tell you: That moment was so embarrassing to me--stealing and the humiliation of taking it back. I made up my mind that I would never steal again. That became my first honest moment. My sponsor was right. I was no longer that person. But I had to see that for myself. I had a conscience. The brain in active addiction does not have a conscience. I was learning that through all of those programs, sessions, exercises and meetings, I had been made into someone brand new. And it was time to live the new Lucy's life and leave the old Lucy's life buried with the old Lucy. It was a big moment for me. Because, in a weird way, my biggest fear did come true. Like I said, old, addicted Lucy died--just like I feared she would--so that the new hopeful Lucy could be born, live and thrive. I was changing right before my eyes. This situation helped me see this clearly.

I continued my recovery programs. I continued my meetings. I continued building and improving my life. I continued my education. I continued to grow into something I could not have ever imagined prior. I stayed in upstate New York and never went back home. Before I knew it God revealed His plan to me and I came to Georgia. In those five years of recovery, God had opened the doors of hell and let me out. God told me to go back and get others from the hell of addiction. Today, I wake up daily to that mission. It's been 30 years. This is what recovery looks like. I just put one foot in the front of the other, one day at a time. I've been doing that since that day I got on a bus to White Plains, NY.

Addict:

A treatment *program* has a beginning and graduation. However "recovery" never ends. You do not want a mindset that produces the question "How long?" Be ready to do whatever you must to win your life back. You don't want to think in terms of beginnings and endings. You want to think in terms of fighting for your life. The question is: *How long will you fight?* The answer should be: *As long as it takes to get it back!* And you must give it away in order to keep it. Those who achieve this permanent mindset are those who will have recovery "permanently."

Recovery is never a goal. Recovery is the practice of a lifestyle. I advise ALL to get really clear on this. This is a daily practice of self-love, self-value and consistent choices that reflect a new and honoring approach to living.

Everyday a person in recovery needs to know (and be able to highlight) what they did for their recovery today. This is an active, intentional and *preventative* way of living. It's an application. It's a practice. For instance, if you ask me--(a person in long-term recovery)--what I did for my recovery today, I may respond: "I exercised. I ate right. I slept properly. I read my bible. I made a difference in another recovering person's life today."--and on and on. For another, this daily lifestyle may mean going to meetings, mountain-climbing, being a great mother, father, grandparent, employee, or going to church or other religious functions. Recovery is about building new habits for living a healthier life all the way around--and doing that daily.

Ally:

To be a powerful ally for your loved one or family member, know the truth about recovery. Know it's more than a program. Know it's a full overhaul in lifestyle. Know these principles. Know them as well as you would if you were learning them to overcome your own addiction. Being an ally means helping the recovering person stay fully present to what recovery truly is 24/7/365 and forever. In the same way that addiction takes over every aspect of a person's life--how they think, live, eat, socialize--everything--recovery should do the same.

You don't want to let your loved one get enchanted by things like "days sober" etc. Those things just don't matter as much as we think. An addict's ability to construct a quality, healthy, habitual lifestyle for their everyday living is forever the goal. If we concentrate on maintaining this, the sobriety days will take care of themselves. This way of seeing things, this way of living the days, builds a security wall between a person in recovery and the possibility of relapse. The best way to be an ally is to never let them lose sight of this. You don't need to badger them; you need to have knowledge--and help provide care and support of a person in recovery. Monitor and encourage their new lifestyle as if it were a medicinal treatment plan--because it is. This lifestyle is *the meds.* The disease must be respected and managed daily.

Clinician:

Addicts certainly have a lifestyle. People in recovery have a lifestyle. Our work as clinicians is to completely help replace one "style" of living with another--while radically changing how a person sees and engages their life--producing a radical behavior modification, leading to a radical shift in their "life results."

I also apply this point of view to those in our new emergency housing program. I am constantly saying to our clients (women and families), "Let this be your last homeless episode." If I see them a week later, I'll say, "So what did you do to end your homelessness today?" If I see them a week later, I might ask, "What did you do to end the possibility of homelessness for yourself today?" With these strategically placed questions, I am gradually shifting a mindset and approach to life. I'm letting them know that they can be the positive cause to overcome the negative effects in their lives. I'm restoring their hope and belief in themselves. We are modifying victim thought and victim behavior.

To Recovery:

In our recovery environment at Mary Hall, we are going to hold your hand through all of the heavy lifting--to help you get to the real achievement--a daily recovered lifestyle. And you'd might as well settle in. Because that is a lifestyle of continued maintenance. By consistently doing this type of incremental work, you'll slowly but surely have less and less problems and issues--less difficulties in life related to active addiction. Things will smooth out. And before you know it, you'll be flying high in life in a way that has nothing to do with substance use. Life will be too good for you to want to check-out on it. You will have adopted a lifestyle change that has you consistently happy, joyous and free.

RECOVERY PEARL:

"Extreme self-care is now my way of life."

Chapter 16

Solving Other Addictions in the Recovery Process

"It's about healing the whole addiction brain."
- Lucy Hall

CHAPTER 16

Solving Other Addictions in the Recovery Process

Addiction is an all encompassing type of disease. It's pervasive. It takes over a person's life in every way. That's because the addiction behavior grows out of an inner defect around the way a person's brain is set up--neurologically. And for some people, that disease makes them get addicted to everything that could possibly make them dependent.

People in recovery are rarely addicted to just one thing. The addiction neurology latches onto everything. When one has this condition in one area, they must stay vigilant and deeply self-aware of all possible destructive habits. Therefore, while detoxing from the main substance that turned life upside-down, it's highly advised recovering addicts seek and find all other smaller addictions hiding in their lives. ALL related issues and behaviors need to be addressed, like smoking, mental-health issues, sex addictions, gambling, excessive eating, and others. If left unchecked, these minor addictions begin to gain strength, and slowly start to pull a young recovered life right back down the drain. Don't leave the pattern alive--anywhere.

Illustration:

After years of being in recovery, I kept discovering more and more things, more substances and habits that had more power in my life than they should. After I detoxed alcohol and cocaine from my system, I soon found other little demons also choking the life out of me. But I didn't know what I didn't know, until I finally knew. And, little by little, I was getting every sign in the world that it was time to do something about them.

One Sunday morning, it was pouring down a *flood* of rain. It was Lent. The more water that fell from the sky, the more I became convinced that without Noah's Ark, I wasn't going to get to my church at all that day. My little Toyota Camry wasn't built for that kind of brutal weather. Continuing to drive was becoming impossible. But I'd come too far to turn back, and still had too far to go, to get to where I wanted to go. When I get to impassable places in life these day, I have one solution: surrender. So I surrendered. I decided to stop at the closest church to worship and praise.

There was a United Methodist Church on Roswell Road. It just so happened to be that I already knew the pastor there--because Mary Hall Freedom House has friends all throughout Atlanta and suburban Atlanta. I've always made it a point to have faith partners to keep us lifted up. And Pastor Mike, of United Methodist Church, never disappoints.

I'll never forget how I walked into that church, soaked from head to toe. I'll never forget how I could barely believe my ears. It was as if the sermon in progress had been hand-written just for me. Pastor Mike stood at the pulpit passionately explaining to the congregation what *Lent* was all about. His voice might as well had been the voice of God speaking directly to me from those stormy clouds hanging over Sandy Springs. Pastor Mike explained that the meaning of Lent was all about penitence, and abstinence, and giving something up. It was all so surreal. Naturally, I pursed my lips together around that point. I knew abstinence, penitence and giving up things. I was a person in recovery from addiction to alcohol and cocaine. So I had already been observing Lent for a long time without knowing it. Right? As far as I was concerned, in recovery, I had been giving up everything--well--almost everything.

The uncompromising words of Pastor Mike began to fall down upon me heavier and heavier. My pride was melting. His sermon was unrelenting. His message was showing no mercy. And that was good. It was that deeper kind of breakdown of The Word that I didn't want to hear, but needed to hear. I could feel it. I knew another layer of the old me was about to be peeled off--no--*ripped* off. In that moment, standing right there in Pastor Mike's church, I asked God *what He wanted me to give up.* He answered immediately in my mind saying, "I want you to give up those cigarettes." Boy oh boy, how I wanted to pretend like I didn't hear that.

Like most, on the brink of freedom from bondage, I started my attempt to negotiate with God about what I had just heard. But those of you who walk in faith already know there is no negotiation with God. There is just obedience. It is the only way to stay in His favor, lest you fall back into demise. However, at that time, honestly, I was still foolishly testing all of that theory out. My crafty mind started saying to God, "Ok God there are 40 days of Lent. That means I can smoke these two last packs of cigarettes--and on my 40th cigarette--I can give them up." If that sounds like nonsense to you, it's because it is and was. But when addicted to something, nonsense makes a whole lotta sense to you. And back then, my little bartering strategy sadly made sense to me. So soon, God was going to knock some more sense into my head.

On the fateful day of my 39th cigarette, my assistant tracked me down to tell me that my prayer partner, Aletha, had been looking for me. That seemed weird. Why was Aletha trying to track me down so hard? I didn't know why exactly Aletha was looking for me so I turned around and started looking for her. When I finally tracked her down, I asked her what she wanted me so urgently for? Aletha proceeded to tell me something that left me completely stumped and overwhelmed. Out of nowhere, my friend Aletha forthrightly says to me, "Sister Lucy, you know God wants you to give up those cigarettes, right?" *Wait! What? Hold on!*

Now, for a little context, you must understand something; I had had no conversation with Aletha, and she was nowhere near me or Sandy Springs when I had my experience at Pastor Mike's service. I had not disclosed anything to anyone--not one living soul. Aletha's words were the continuation of God's words booming and thundering from the sky. That's how deeply they impacted me. I just stared at her blankly. Then, I stared some more, and probably some more. The 40th cigarette was immediately abandoned. I tossed it. I never smoked again. That was over 25 years ago. And let me tell you something more; after discarding that 40th cigarette I found a whole new layer of my power. I found a new layer of my surrender. I found mansions of new freedom all over my life. I wasn't being owned by things anymore. I was being owned by My Maker and Maker alone--God!

It felt and feels...so good.

Freedom.

Addict:

The more you understand what addiction truly is, you become less afraid to search and find all the places it might be alive in your life. It's not a character defect; it's a disease like any other disease. It spreads. It gains power in all areas of your living--if you let it--if you don't stop it in its tracks.

The disease of addiction ran so deep in my family, I had layers and layers of addictions to shed. And, in my case, I had to turn those layers of bondage into layers of surrender. Not only had I been held hostage to crack-cocaine and alcohol, but I was being held captive by those cigarettes. And after God helped me beat all three of those, I had to face another dire addiction--FOOD.

People who see me today are amazed to learn that I walked into my own recovery program weighing 286 whopping pounds. It was time to do something about that. As this newly "commissioned woman" my entire life was being given a makeover by God. My life was now re-purposed for the greater good and higher calling. I was to be an embodied example of hope for others. As a part of that conviction, I lost 100 pounds. By God's grace and guidance, my total relationship to food radically changed. After these early victories, I felt unstoppable. If He could give me the will, the strength and the instruction to break free from drugs and alcohol, anything was possible with commitment. I started looking for every other bond in my life. God helped me put them all on notice. You can do this too. With help... you can do this.

Ally:

Addictions are hardest to see for those who are drowning in them. When dealing with an addicted loved one, you must understand that fact. They will need all of the support you can show them. Give plenty of patience and your persistent compassion.

When a loved one in recovery starts to shed a world of addictions from their life: cigarettes, junk food, toxic mates, pornography, gambling, you might need to shed some as well. This can be a powerful way of showing your support. If you can detox those lesser "lifestyle addictions" which may be operating in your life also, it helps the recovering person to maintain the cleaner living environment needed to hold their newly recovered life together. And don't worry. If they can break highly addictive habits like cocaine or heroin use, surely you can give up smoking to help them maintain the same. This is how you can be an ally to someone in recovery. This is how you be an ally to self.

Clinician:

All have addictions. All have unhealthy habits they need to be rid of. And from my observation, I have not seen enough addiction recovery specialists who are deeply interested in personal health and well-being for themselves. I think I also appeared this way in the early days of my career. I was digging myself out from a hole so deep, my progress in health looked like someone else's failings in health.

Bottom line is this: as a practitioner, If I'm sitting in a session, running a session, teaching the session, and it's clear that I should be the chief attendee of the session, there's a problem. The way I approach the people I counsel today is with a mindset that says, "I can only take you as far as I've gone."

I always suggest clinicians and facilities adopt this same mindset. It can only change your life for the good. Be an inspiration to those you are helping, just by example. A healthcare clinician's first and foremost job should be providing health "care" to themselves. We shouldn't speak of bringing transformation into the lives of others, if we are unwilling to transform our own. Don't be another kind of addict (on the down-low) trying to help others overcome their addictions to opioids, cocaine or alcohol. Some of us may not be owned by those addictive substances today, but we may be wholly owned by caffeine, nicotine, sugar or even the drama of an abusively bad relationship. We need to cut that out ASAP. *Why?* Because addiction is addiction. It's the same ill-brain caught in the same ill trap.

This whole journey of recovery is about journeying toward ever improving health--is it not? Addiction is a healthcare issue. And we, as clinicians, should refuse to carry legal addictions that are diminishing our wellbeing. You might think your addiction is not as bad as another's addiction--but again--addiction is addiction, health is health, wellbeing is wellbeing. Let's get serious about this work. Let's *be* this work.

Recovery:

At Mary Hall, our program is about detoxing the whole mentality of addiction, not just the drug or substance itself. We are trying to get rid of the very root of use. Whether it was inherited or developed by lifestyle, we want to uproot the very neurology of addiction behavior. The power of recovery makes this possible; recover every part of your life that the addiction mind has controlled.

RECOVERY PEARL:

"The root of addiction has many branches. Chop them all down."

Chapter 17

How to Become a Recovery Counselor or Peer

"Some of the best clinicians are former addicts."

- Lucy Hall

CHAPTER 17

How to Become a Recovery Counselor or Peer

I encourage those saved from this disease to save others from its grips. Helping others helps you keep recovery alive in yourself--creating another line of defense. This chapter illustrates how many recovering people are choosing successful careers in the field of addiction recovery. Having been there personally makes you a powerful beacon of hope for others. If you feel that calling, answer it. It is a powerful mission. Drug abuse often spreads through peer-to-peer introductions. The eradication of drug abuse can happen the same way.

Illustration:

The life I live today is such a privilege and such a surprise. You may not understand. I was a down and out addict who had been arrested and given the choice between jail or treatment in New York. I chose the latter and it became the ladder. I was in program after program for a year because I was willing to listen to others and go to any lengths to get this newfound recovery life. I went from detox to in-patient treatment, to halfway house. I did not know where I was going; I just knew I didn't want to go backwards. My A.A. sponsor at that time told me to come work at a treatment center as a volunteer. *Okay. Sure! Why not?* It was a place called St. Peter's Rehabilitation Center, in Rotterdam, NY. My sponsor worked there in a finance position. She did not want me (a young recovering person) to have idle time on my hands. She wanted me to have something to do so that I would not relapse in any shape, form or fashion. I already had a good momentum going and she wanted me to keep that. So did I. I accepted. I went. I volunteered.

Within 30-days that treatment program offered me the overnight monitor position. A job. I remember that I worked for a guy name Mike. I oversaw the men's unit of the treatment facility. I do remember it being an easy job, because everyone was sleep. I was just there on-call for emergencies. Then things changed. Big time. My manager changed. My job changed. *Easy* changed.

In my new job, I still worked overnight, and at the very same facility, but this time I sat over the women's unit--all night. It was literally like night and day compared to my previous post. It was there that I learned a big difference between men and women in recovery. I would no longer be able to just coast through the night. My job had just turned into a *job*. Same job, different gender, different worlds. When I worked on the men's unit, everything was way, way, super easy. *Why?* Men went to bed, stayed in bed, then got up in the morning and just did what they needed to do. Women, on the other hand, got up in the middle of the night--A LOT-- crying over breakups with boyfriends, crying because something physically hurt, crying because of something with their children, crying because they were dealing with the legal system, etc. Women just did not sleep all night long. They always had drama and compound drama. That was a huge eye-opener for me.

The women who were up at night were always coming to me for a variety of issues. They turned me into a counselor. I had to stay up all night to give them guidance and encouragement. And by God's grace, I was very helpful to them. It's absolutely amazing when I think back. Fate is intelligent. God is knowing. I would have never discovered my purpose had I continued to sit over that men's unit. Most of the guys, I just would never see. I never really had to. They were sleep. They never came to sit and talk and work out their problems. And with the women, there was just never a dull night. From 11pm to 7am, I knew we had to get through whatever came up. If I needed to stop and pray with someone for almost an hour, that's what I did. I learned early on that the key was to deeply listen, then prayerfully give sound advice or encouragement. I would share my experiences, strength and hope. It was becoming clear that I had a knack for this. At a certain point, I solidly realized this was the type of work I was supposed to do. It all just kind of happened.

Not long after, I learned about a government grant offering funding to train people to get their credentials as recovery counselors. As soon as I found out about it, I enrolled. I did all of the courses. Soon after, I was officially credentialed. I got my C.A.C. (Credentialed Alcohol & Drug Addiction Counselor).

I soon took a second job working at the Schenectady Alcohol & Drug Counsel. I worked for a Mr. Smith. I learned a lot about the kind of boss I did not want to be, but still, I learned a lot from that man. I still use some of his sayings until this very day. One of his sayings I use with my employees is, "If you are going to wear your feelings on your sleeves, wear short sleeves." He didn't want drama in his organization. He made it clear he did not care about your feelings when it came to getting the job done. He just needed the job done. I have a lot more compassion than good old Mr. Smith. That man was an interesting piece of work. He did me more good than bad. He served his divine purpose in my life. God bless his heart and the heart of anyone still dealing with him on a daily basis.

It was while working at Schenectady Alcohol & Drug Counsel that I journeyed to Georgia to visit my brother. And that's when I fell in love with Atlanta. It was so beautiful. The weather was so beautiful. There was no snow–no cold. I had just left a place where there was snow up to my waist, and it was January. I was sold. My brother and his family were doing very well for themselves. I was inspired. I was amazed to see so many affluent black people doing extremely well. Good ol' Mr. Smith made it easy to consider Atlanta as well. Anyone in the right mind could only take but so much of him. When I returned from Atlanta, I started talking to God and saying my goodbyes to the state of New York. And by September of that year I had moved to Georgia and already had another counseling job. I was a career woman now. I was (and am) a Recovery Counselor.

Addict:

I love it when former addicts aspire to be recovery counselors or peers. People in recovery respond powerfully to people who have been where they currently are. It inspires REAL HOPE and faith that they can claw their way out of hell too. I've consulted with many women who have graduated from Mary Hall Freedom House, women who have reinvented their lives and now want to run their own programs. They have a pay-it-forward mindset just as I did when I began the recovery life. Just today, I was working with three of these individuals, giving consultation about their programs. I shared a lot of the same wisdom and principles I've shared here. What I'm finding is that a lot of times young founders are very eager--which is a good thing--but often want to rush the process instead of go through the appropriate paces, in the appropriate time. However, we first must develop ourselves into the people we need to be to fulfill these dreams. I may have also been this way when I was younger. I can't remember. But it doesn't matter and it didn't matter. The development process could not be circumvented. I had to go through it. I'm a better woman for it. I'm a better counselor for it. And it also anchored me in my recovery lifestyle in a way that I don't think anything else could have. For that reason alone, I think more people in recovery should consider becoming trained professionals in the field. Saving other's lives deepens the saving of your own.

There are several educational routes for getting into the field of recovery as a professional. Some seek out online schools, community colleges or universities that offer Associate Degree, Bachelor Degree and Masters Degree programs. But others start their educational journeys by first getting industry certification certificates--depending upon the licensing offered per state. For example there are certification programs to become a Peer Recovery Support Specialist, National Certified Adolescent Addictions Counselor, National Certified Addiction Counselor. Taking volunteer jobs in the industry also helps to build your resume and experience. That's the route I took; then I gradually began coursework to gather industry credentials.

Ally:

Recovery makes miracles possible for former addicts. I had no idea God would raise me to become a professional ally for sufferers of addiction. The possibility was the furthest from my mind or the mind of anyone who knew me growing up. But sometimes life has a mind of its own. If your loved ones return from a program wanting to enter the recovery field as a counselor or peer, do all you can to support them. It's one of the healthiest routes they can take to maintain the recovery lifestyle.

Over twenty years ago I started a little community program to help fellow recovering people. I called it *Mary Hall* Freedom House, the name of my mother and my daughter. All I had was a high-school education and a big heart. Today I am a CEO with a bustling staff of miracle working hope dealers. The recovery program at Mary Hall Freedom House has a multi-million dollar budget, recovers hundreds of women each year and is renowned. Over ten-thousand sisters have come through our doors for recovery! Can you imagine all of the renewed lives? When I began the Freedom House, I was only six years into my own recovery. Currently, we serve 240 women and 80 children every single day, with many different types of programs. And though we started as the Mary Hall Freedom "House," we have been rapidly becoming the Mary Hall Freedom "Village." And yes, the demand is such that we need more. Our program is a continuum of care for recovering women and their families--aiming to treat the *whole life.* And it amazes me right unto this very day. Who would have thought? I didn't see it coming. I was an addict who just surrendered, listened, and obeyed. My ever budding faith in Him, restored me personally, and guided me to this point, to restore others. Who else but God, could have done this? I to all of you unbelievers: I sure couldn't.

My message then, and now, to all who enter our doors is simple: *"If He did it for me, He will do it for you. I was no more worthy of His grace than you. I had fallen to the lowest of the low, and now all the freedom I have, so can you. Trust me, take my hand, and we'll see you through!"*

Clinician:

People see my success and want to be where I am today--instantly. But (oh my God) they really shouldn't want that. I cannot tell you how thankful I am that all of these responsibilities and resources were not thrust upon me before time--before I had developed the skills, maturity, experiences and know-how to handle them properly. Ask the people who have known me a long time. I was kind of a mess when I first started. I just was. But I didn't stay that way. I worked to become who I needed to be so that this vision could live in the world in a real and effective way. But know this: even when I was a mess, I still held this vision. I still KNEW the mission. It was clear. It was concise. It was written down, powerful and fired me up everyday. Once I accepted my purpose in life, I knew exactly where I wanted to go. I just didn't know "the how." And I didn't yet know how I to become "the who." Today we are growing by great leaps. So am I, as a person.

Since the beginning, my vision for this recovery enterprise has always been about a "village." That vision has been my *true north* through it all. Everyday I knew exactly where we were attempting to go. And 20 years later, the village is coming to pass. But, entrepreneurs, listen to me: I could not do what we are doing today at year 3, or year 6, or year 10 of this enterprise. Why? Because, I was not ready. I still had to grow. And that's exactly what I did--I grew me--and this facility, through all of its phases and my phases. That's the process. It was a process that could not be skipped. And here we are.

To Recovery:

Lastly... Though I had a vision, though I had a stated mission, everything that we are, everything that we have, and everything that we do today is so much bigger than I could have imagined. It is a God thing. I've been His project under construction for 30 years. That's where I give the credit because that is just the real of the real.

I aspire to help others get started in this field. If you want to do what I do, and if you ever should meet me, be completely prepared to tell me your vision in "one powerful sentence." I can't wait to hear it. I can't wait to help. Helping others get free is the best way to strengthen your own freedom from this disease. For more certification information on entering this field, go to www.Naadac.org Or, if you want us to help you start a Freedom Village in your city, contact me: LucyHall@MHFH.org today.

RECOVERY PEARL:

"Helping others recover, helps you recover."

Chapter 18

Is Society's Drug Crisis Solvable?

"We have lost the War on Drugs, because we tried to wage war on a *disease*."

- Lucy Hall

CHAPTER 18

Is Society's Drug Crisis Solvable?

I've never been as encouraged about the possibility of solving the drug crisis than the day I heard about *The Portugal Experiment.* It so impressed me. While America continues to treat the problem of addiction as a crime, there are other societies beginning to take more enlightened approaches from more enlightened points of view. And you know what? They are achieving mind-blowing, phenomenal results. Can we not "also" be enlightened to lighten the burden on our society? I think we can.

Illustration:

As I write this, America is going through a deadly opioid and heroin epidemic. Reports say that in the 1990s, the nation of Portugal went through one of their own. Droves of people died due to heroin addiction. Overdoses were rampant and all too common. The epidemic was affecting everyone. Today, family trees in Lisbon, Portugal are missing countless branches due to this tidal wave of deaths from the 1990s. It was like a country at war with itself, via addiction.

Originally trying to fight this problem the old-fashioned way, by criminalization and penalization (and getting absolutely nowhere), Portugal's legislators decided to take a different approach. A radically different approach. It became known as The Portugal experiment. In 2001, the country decriminalized all drugs across the board--yes, cocaine, heroin, everything.

Criminal cases instantly became medical cases. Addiction went from being seen as an attack on society to a chronic disease that afflicted citizens were suffering from--worthy of compassion. Addicts went from being treated with scorn to being treated empathy. Amazing.

People caught with less than a 10-day supply of any illicit drug are sent to something called a Commission for the Dissuasion of Drug Addiction. They say it's a commission of 3 people: a social worker, a lawyer and a doctor. They would decide what the government will do with the person caught, and the vast majority of the time, reports say the person was almost always sent to free treatment. Reports say the government began dispatching medical officials, dispensing Methadone to addicts on the street to help slowly break their heroin addictions. Free, clean needles were being given out everywhere. The government maintained its policy to provide free treatment and counseling to those who wanted it, but the people were no longer being penalized for drug use.

Many, especially in America, would think the mass decriminalization of all of these hardcore drugs would have turned Portugal, or any nation, into a wild drug infested country of crazed addicts. After all, people could freely use heroin or cocaine as casually as eating a hamburger. Wouldn't a civilized society break down into complete chaos? No--it didn't happen that way.

15 years after The Portugal Experiment, reports say heroin use dropped by 75%, the overdose rate fell by 85%, the spread of AIDS/HIV via drug needles dropped by 95% (after the government started dispensing clean needles to addicts), and deaths via heroin sank to all time lows. It's said Portugal's drug mortality rate became the lowest in all of Western Europe. How amazing is that? Their counterintuitive approach has saved countless lives, saved their government countless dollars, and restored countless families.

America's war still rages. The result? Overdose rates are rising to record highs. But leading thinkers say it's obvious that Portugal won their War on Drugs by ending it. Compassion and medical treatment became the government's socially *rational* and fiscally *rational* solution to their drug crisis.

Addict:

To all who struggle with addiction, I say one thing: Have hope. I truly believe help is on the way in a massive form. **The world is starting to realize that you are not a criminal but a victim of a neurological and biochemical health challenge. New research everyday is proven this to be a brain disease--and one that can be managed.** "I love you." That's all I've been trying to say from first page to last. I see you. I know this disease is not who you truly are. I was once buried beneath this disease. But someone had to see me. Someone had to notice my hand reaching out from that grave. Someone had to know that I could be more. Someone had to love me until I could love myself.

If you've seen yourself reflected anywhere in these pages, in anyway, I pray your survival instincts kick-in before it's too late. I pray you find the strength to realize, admit and heal. Come save yourself. I know the pathway. I emerged from a grave to greatness, by God's grace. It wasn't easy, but YOU CAN DO THIS TOO. You don't have to live that way, beloved. And you certainly don't have to die that way. Transformation is possible. Don't be embarrassed. This is a medical issue. You've just fallen sick. And now, either you're going to choose to get better, or *consciously* choose to get sicker. But after talking to me, you won't be getting sicker out of ignorance or oblivion. It's going to be a choice. My advice: surrender and survive. Again, *"I love you."* Come. Let's save your life.

Ally:

Meanwhile, America still spends billions of dollars chasing, penalizing and incarcerating its citizenry for what leading thinkers and new research is concluding is a medical issue? We need real allies today. Political ones. We need enlightened legislators to be the allies of the drug crisis. The hawkish ones have had their way. They need to let go of the reins. It's really time for us to be BIG ENOUGH to finally admit: our War on Drugs has been a dismal failure. And, in my opinion (and the opinion of a lot of other professionals), it has exacerbated the crisis. I know we can create something better for our collective future. We now have the knowledge, we just need people in power with the courage.

In America, most see the drug problem as a perpetual drama that will never end. There seems to always be a new generation born into lives infused with trauma: soldiers returning traumatized from war, citizens traumatized from living in urban blight, or children with parents too busy chasing money to build enriching emotional bonds--leaving children emotionally traumatized (or sexually traumatized after being left with the wrong person) and now also wanting to escape their lives. Drugs are available to all who want to escape the pains of living. Then the authorities go to war with users and dealers, creating mass incarceration, breaking millions of families--and a new round of trauma begins from the fallout of that--dispensing new reasons for affected citizens to pick up. Where does it end? I think it ends with a complete change of mind. We have been looking at this problem the wrong way.

One day I stumbled across a powerful, powerful TED talk. When I tell you it blew me away, I mean it blew me away. It was so enlightening. It was so intriguing. It was a TED talk by Johnathan Hari about the roots of addiction. The talk was entitled: "Everything You Think You Know About Addiction is Wrong." You already know Lucy Hall was going to click on that. I'm so glad I did. I advise everyone who has ever dealt with addiction, personally, or by relationship, to click on it at TED.com. It verifies so much of what I've seen and experienced over time as an Addiction Specialist, a former addict, and a member of a family which has been ravaged by addiction related deaths.

Mr. Hari begins his talk speaking of a childhood experience where he remembers being unable to wake one of his relatives. At the time he did not understand why. But when he became older, he learned that the disease of addiction ran in his family. Struggling to figure out how to truly help people he loved (who were addicts) led him on a fascinating quest to understand addiction, and its solution, in a completely different way. I recommend every addicted person, family member, clinician and legislator watch the 15 minute video. There is a new way to see this thing. The solution to addiction isn't what you think it is.

Arming ourselves with these new perspectives and ways of approach, in my opinion, is the only way to solve the drug crisis. I can't do this on my own with my center in Atlanta, Georgia. WE NEED HELP ACROSS THE BOARD. I think this latest epidemic has a lot more people ready to help. Addiction is no longer something that is "out there" with "those people." And perhaps it never was. The opioid crisis is touching everyone–every socio-economic group in America. An addict is no longer a stereotype on TV or a street corner on the wrong side of town, it's your daughter who went to all the right private schools. Let's do something. We can become allies today.

Clinician:

We've got a lot of work to do. And I want to help all do it to the best of their abilities. We must innovate our approach. People need us now more than ever. WHEN I LOOK OUT AT PEOPLE STRUGGLING in other recovery programs, the threats to their longterm success are clear to me. Most have not been empowered by strategically seeking and discovering their needs. Most have not been empowered by digging, exhuming and employing their voice. Most have not been empowered by drawing out their life map to know where they are going in their newly decided lives. Most have not been empowered by finding a safe enough community or person with which to share their fall-backs and transgressions. And, in my professional opinion, for true success, these components must be discovered along the journey of recovery if it's going to be a long-term victory.

For those care-providers who want to emulate our success in the field, know this; I have one "quality metric" from which I run my facility, and it's really simple. Here it is: "I would not ask the ladies in my care to live anywhere that I would not live." That is my metric for quality when it comes to Mary Hall Freedom Village. My metric for healthcare services is a similar declaration. "I would not subject recovery participants to a level of subpar treatment that would have never given me longterm freedom from my own addictions." It's a good rule to function by.

To Recovery:

Whether an addicted person, loved-one of an addicted person, clinician, legislator or politician looking to affect policy, I hope these pages have contributed to your insights on the matter. I really believe we can do a lot to turn this disease around--as well as turn around the statistics--and the toll addiction takes on our world. So many lives hang in the balance. Please. Stand with me. Let's be good samaritans together. Sometimes, that's all it takes to save a life.

RECOVERY PEARL:

"With enlightenment, we can solve this."

SUMMARIES

Chapter 1

Who is an Addict?

Acknowledging and admitting can be the hardest step to recovery, but it's the first and most pivotal. Societal shame keeps many un-admitted addicts in complete stasis--away from the recovery help that could save them and put their lives back in POWER. I was in this dark hole for years. This chapter discusses how to drop deadly pride and shame, get honest, get clean and get healthy again.

Chapter 2

Why Do People Abuse Drugs?

People mainly abuse for reasons rooted in life trauma. It's no coincidence so many war veterans, people with hard economic lives or brutal emotional lives, become addicts. Even people experiencing medical trauma become vulnerable to chemical addiction. All are seeking escape and relief of pain. This chapter illustrates how trauma and addiction are linked.

Chapter 3

Gateway Drugs: Myth or Reality?

Short answer: "Yes." There is a such thing as a gateway drug. Many romance the notion that recreational drug use is harmless, but repeated use can set off a chain-reaction. I started with weed and ended with chronic alcoholism and crack-addiction. Tons have the same story. This chapter shows why any addictive substance can eventually spark the addiction neurology.

Chapter 4

Is My Teen Getting High?

The teen years are difficult for child and parent alike, but adding addiction to the mix makes things volatile real quick. Once a child leaves your home they're exposed to every societal ill--including drugs, addicted peers and dealers. Kids' rebellious experimentations can sometimes go badly, and even prove fatal. This chapter illustrates signs to look for before it's too late.

Chapter 5

How to Survive an Overdose

The best way to survive an overdose is not to have one--get treatment; stop using. If you or someone else is in overdose, call 911 immediately! The person likely only has minutes before the overdose becomes a fatality. So many will not survive! Learn the overdose signs and counteractive techniques and overdose prevention substances you should have on hand to save a life during overdose in this chapter.

Chapter 6

When Addiction Turns Violent or Criminal

Addict mentality: nothing or no one is more important than getting high. An addict's life is organized around the goal of getting high. If you're an obstacle to this goal, an addict could become physically violent. Addicts might steal property or sell their bodies to financially support the habit. This chapter lets loved ones know when, how, or if to get law enforcement involved.

Chapter 7

I Gotta Hit Rock-Bottom to Change?

Bottom is a powerful catalyst to change. It turns your life around or kills you. I hit it. I survived mine. Many do not. Rock-bottom is when you've fallen so low you cannot fall any further. Most think you can't fall any lower than the grave, but you can--like dragging a child or mate into the pit of hell with you. This chapter discusses deciding to change before losing the option.

Chapter 8

How to Stage a Successful Intervention?

Intervention is not *confrontation*. Being confrontational is the opposite of what you should be when encouraging an addict to seek help. Remembering addiction is a chronic brain disease is key. Would you be confrontational or compassionate toward a loved one with advanced stages of cancer? Firm, but loving is the way. This chapter helps create better intervention results.

Chapter 9

Detox vs. Recovery: The Difference?

Detox is detoxification of your blood, not eliminating the (brain-disorder) disease of addiction. *Recovery* as a program manages and shuts down the power of the addiction disease on a day-to-day basis. It builds your entire living to make you powerful (instead of powerless) in the face of addiction neurology. This life-saving chapter breaks down the crucial difference.

Chapter 10

Help! They Took My Kids!

Once DFACS takes your children, you're going to need help. Don't lose hope. Don't sink even deeper into abusing from depression and guilt. I've been there. I recovered. I got my baby back. Getting children back from foster care can be exceedingly hard, and my facility specializes in this. In this chapter I talk about what you will need to fight for your family.

Chapter 11

What to Do After Detox?

Answer: Run to the nearest long-term recovery program. Completion of a detox program is not a recovered life. Detox only readies you to tackle the real work of fully recovering your life. Mistakenly thinking you're healed after a few weeks makes you a prime candidate for relapse. This chapter illustrates what *true recovery* is, before addiction returns with more ferocity.

Chapter 12

How to Avoid a Relapse?

This disease deserves your constant vigilance and respect. Underestimating it can be deadly. Five or fifty years sober is no cause to get relaxed about your disease. Should a surviving cancer patient suddenly stop the healthy lifestyle activity helping keep their cancer in remission and them alive? This chapter breaks down how and why to remain vigilant about this baffling, cunning and complex disease.

Chapter 13

Helping Loved Ones in Recovery

Addicts need a secret life to support their secret (or not so secret) addictions. Signs are always there for alert family, friends and loved ones. Abrupt changes in behavioral pattern or personality are always first indication. When a person becomes more withdrawn, erratic, compulsive or secretive, something's going on. This chapter tells you all to look for.

Chapter 14

Fixing Relationships Addiction Destroyed

Most addictions deal with mind altering substances, causing severe mental impairment and compromised judgement. The things we do while under the influence can be horrific--to self and to others. Repairing key relationships can be the hardest work in a new life of recovery. This chapter illustrates just how hard that work can be, but why we must persist.

Chapter 15

Complete Recovery Takes How Long?

A recovered life is not a program you start and end; it is a total overhaul of who a person is and how a person lives from the inside out. Addiction eventually takes over every aspect of a person's life--how they think, live, eat, socialize--everything. Recovery should do the same. This chapter illustrates what a life in recovery looks like on a day-to-day basis.

Chapter 16

Solving Other Addictions in the Recovery Process

Most fixate on the substances addicts get addicted to; we focus on the traumatized soul who gets addicted to them. If you do not treat the damaged *addiction brain*, you will soon swap out one addiction scenario for another, because the compulsive abuse of things becomes the way you do life. Finding lesser addictions operating in your life is key. This chapter discusses it.

Chapter 17

How to Become a Recovery Counselor or Peer

I encourage those saved from this disease to save others from its grips. Helping others helps you keep recovery alive in yourself, creating another line of defense. This chapter illustrates how many recovering addicts are choosing successful careers in the field of addiction recovery. Having been there personally makes you a powerful beacon of hope for others.

Chapter 18

Is Society's Drug Crisis Solvable?

The war on drugs has been a dismal failure. The punitive approach on what is truly a medical disease has not only been proven unethical, and merciless, but illogical. Other societies are becoming more enlightened about addiction and addiction treatment, drastically reducing their addiction statistics with new and innovative approaches. This chapter discusses new hope.